MATTER MINER

Matter Miner

**RAY WRIGHT
JACOBS**

Staten House

Prologue

You've probably heard the saying, "To be successful, one must mind their own business." While there's truth in that, I propose that lasting success requires more than just minding—it demands that we **Mine** the vast wisdom available to us, much like a Bitcoin miner diligently solves complex algorithms to earn newly minted coins. Just as the miner invests effort and resources to unlock new wealth, we must delve deep into the reservoirs of knowledge and insight to shape the **Matter** of our heart's desires into reality.

Welcome to "**Matter Miner: Immutable Laws That Attract Success with Every Thought.**" This book is a journey into the heart of thought mastery and its profound impact on personal and professional success. As you turn these pages, you embark on a transformative path that redefines the conventional understanding of what it means to succeed.

In our world, the notion that 'you are what you think' has never been more relevant. Yet, while many acknowledge this principle in passing, few grasp its depth and fewer still harness its full potential. Here, we delve into the immutable laws that govern the universe—laws that do not change or waver, but consistently respond to the frequencies emitted by our thoughts.

This book is not merely about thinking positively but about thinking purposefully. It is about aligning your mental frequencies with the vibrations of abundance and destiny. Through the pages of this book, you will learn how to fine-tune your mind to attract the life you not only desire but are destined to live.

Each chapter is designed to guide you through understanding and applying these laws—providing you with practical tools and strategies to transform your thought patterns. From uncovering the mechanics of the Law of Attraction to learning how to apply these principles consistently and effectively, you will discover how to use your mental power to influence your reality.

You will explore how successful individuals harness these laws to create opportunities, overcome obstacles, and achieve their dreams. This book invites you to shift your perspective from passive observer to active creator, from someone who hopes for change to someone who manifests it.

As we journey through these principles together, remember that the power to change your life lies within your thoughts. Each thought is a seed planted in the fertile soil of the universe, and with the right knowledge and application, you can grow a garden of endless possibilities.

Prepare to unlock the doors to a new realm of potential, where your thoughts are not just fleeting whispers in the wind but powerful forces that shape your reality. Welcome to "Matter Miner: Immutable Laws That Attract Success with Every Thought." Let's begin this 14 Chapter journey together, and may every thought you cultivate bring you closer to the abundance and success you seek.

Ray Wright Jacobs

INTRODUCTION

Welcome to *Matter Miner*, where every thought you entertain holds the potential to transform your life. This book isn't just another fleeting attempt at self-improvement; it's a master key to unlocking the true power that exists within you—a power designed by God and accessible through His divine laws. Imagine being able to mine the Mind of Christ, much like a prospector discovers gold, extracting the precious elements of thought and turning them into the building blocks of success, purpose, and abundance. That's what *Matter Miner* is all about. It's a guide to digging deep into the unseen forces of how your thoughts aligned them with God's will, can manifest the life you've always been destined for.

This is not some surface-level self-help manual. It's a blueprint for anyone who has grown tired of the shallow promises offered by popular culture. Here, you'll discover the *Dynamic Laws of the Universe*, unshakable truths that govern how your thoughts, words, and actions are actually received images that create your reality. These laws are not just philosophical ideas; they are divine absolutes that, when properly understood and applied, unlock the door to limitless possibilities. With each chapter, you'll come to understand how mastering these laws leads to true transformation—both spiritually and materially.

At the heart of *Matter Miner* is the dynamic law of *NOW Faith*—an active, present-tense law that requires your belief, in order to propel your desires into reality. This faith is not a passive hope but a dynamic force that works in the now, shaping your future with every thought and declaration. It's this immediate faith that separates wishful thinking from divine manifestation. You'll learn how to harness it, how to move from intention to action, and how to witness the profound shift that occurs when your life is aligned with God's immutable truth.

This book doesn't just tell you *what* to do; it shows you *how* to do it. You'll walk away with practical strategies for transforming thought into action, breaking free from the strongholds that have kept you bound in fear and doubt, and stepping into a reality shaped by divine abundance. You'll also learn that action rooted in divine guidance is the true catalyst for manifestation, not the frantic hustle that the world glorifies. Each step you take, each move you make in NOW faith, brings you closer to the extraordinary life God has promised.

But NOW faith without action is incomplete. This book goes beyond the basics of belief and dives into the importance of NOW faith aligned movements, that unlock God's promises and bring about miraculous manifestations in your life. It's not about chasing success, but rather about positioning yourself to receive it. By aligning with divine laws, you'll step into a flow where the universe itself supports and amplifies your every move.

You'll also learn about the *Power of Thought Frequency*, an understanding that bridges science and spirituality. Every thought you think attracts like thoughts and sends out a frequency that shapes the world around you. By tapping into this power, you become an active participant in co-creating your reality. Whether it's breaking free from mental strongholds or manifesting your desires, *Matter Miner* gives you the tools to rewire your thought patterns and align them with the divine blueprint for success.

Matter Miner is your invitation to go beyond the ordinary, to dig deeper into the subconscious mind, where the frequencies of faith and thought converge to create the world around you. It's time to rise above the limitations of your Sarx-driven nature and embrace the truth that all of heaven's resources are at your disposal when you align with God's laws. The universe is waiting for your next move. Will you mine the Matter tucked deep in your divinely inspired thoughts and step into the limitless potential that awaits? This is your moment. Let's begin.

UNDERSTANDING THE FREQUENCIES OF THE TWO REALMS

In every human being, two distinct realms of thought coexist, each functioning on its own unique frequency: the Conscious Mind and the Subconscious Mind. Much like the difference between AM and FM radio signals, these two frequencies are undetectable to each other. The Conscious Mind operates at a surface level, seated in the brain of the human skull. It processes information through the five senses—what we see, hear, touch, taste, and smell—making it primarily concerned with physical reality, immediate responses, and survival. It reacts to the external world, but it is bound by logic, fear, doubt, and limitations. This mind is often preoccupied with worry, imagination, and reasoning, distracted by the noise of the world around it.

In contrast, the Subconscious Mind operates on a much higher frequency, residing in the heart. This is the realm where divine wisdom flows, where faith, intuition, and discernment live. The Subconscious Mind transcends the noise of the physical world and taps into the infinite potential of the spiritual realm. It is through this mind that the Wonderful Counselor—the Holy Spirit—delivers guidance, wisdom, and images of success. While the Conscious Mind may struggle with doubt and fear, the Subconscious Mind accepts only the thoughts and convictions that are deeply rooted in faith. It's here, at this higher frequency, where our thoughts are transformed into reality.

CONSCIOUS MIND	SUBCONSCIOUS MIND
Flesh	*Spirit*
5-Sense Sensory Input	*Spiritually Discerned Attunement*
Pain-Pleasure Responsive	*NOW Faith Conviction Activated*
Master	*Servant*
Operates: Conscious Realm	*Operates: Subconscious Realm*
Location: Brain of Human Skull	*Location: Brain of Human Heart*
Fear-Worry	*Love-Meditation*
Reason-Wishing	*Discernment-Prayer*
Imagination-Planning	*Intuition-Knowing*
Will Power	*Image Acceptance*
Short-Term Imperfect Memory	*Long-Term Perfect Memory*
Temporary Storage (RAM)	*Permanent Storage (ROM)*

However, there is a constant battle between these two realms. The Conscious Mind, weighed down by the distractions of the physical world, can easily disrupt the spiritual process of manifestation when fear, doubt, or impatience creeps in. These negative thoughts interfere with the blessings and guidance that God has already set into motion, causing a delay or even a cancellation of the promises meant for us. It's when we allow the frequency of the lower Conscious Mind to dominate that we open ourselves to loss—blessings stolen by external forces, both seen and unseen, who thrive on our doubt and hesitation.

To unlock the full power of your potential, you must learn to guard your thoughts and keep your Subconscious Mind attuned to the higher spiritual frequency, where God's guidance resides. Praise, prayer, worship, and spiritual warfare are not just actions or rituals but are tools, each uniquely designed to attune us to those higher frequencies. Each one of these practices operates at a deeper level of spiritual engagement and communication, unlocking different aspects of God's divine power and presence in our lives.

Praise, for instance, is the most immediate and accessible form of worship. It focuses on recognizing the goodness of God, expressed through thanksgiving, joy, and declarations of His glory. When we praise, we speak life into our circumstances and draw near to God's presence. Praise lifts us above our problems and shifts our focus from earthly limitations to divine possibilities. It opens a spiritual channel, allowing us to experience the manifestation of God's joy and strength. In this realm, we align our Conscious Mind to the truth that God is greater than any challenge. This act, in itself, is a form of warfare because it repels the forces of discouragement, fear, and doubt that seek to inhabit our thoughts.

Prayer, on the other hand, is a more intimate and focused dialogue with the Creator. It's the process of speaking directly to God, making our requests known, interceding for others, and offering our hearts in supplication. Through prayer, we engage not only with the Conscious Mind but also with the Subconscious, as true prayer moves beyond words and into the deeper places of the spirit. It is here that the faithful believer brings petitions to the throne, trusting that God, in His infinite wisdom, will respond. Prayer serves as a tool for aligning our desires with His will, connecting the two realms of our mind, and bridging the gap between human limitation and divine possibility.

Worship transcends both praise and prayer. It is a full surrender, a heart posture where we lay down every ounce of our being before God, acknowledging His sovereignty. Worship is the act of total submission, where we quiet the noise of the Conscious Mind and allow our Subconscious Mind to rise into the presence of God. In this space, we encounter the raw essence of His glory. This is where transformation happens, where the image of Christ is impressed upon our hearts, and where we receive divine revelation. Worship taps into the deeper frequency of the spiritual realm, allowing us to access the blueprint of heaven for our lives, relationships, and callings.

Finally, **spiritual warfare** is the active defense and offense we must employ to maintain our place in the Kingdom. The Bible says that "we wrestle not against flesh and blood but against principalities, powers, and rulers of darkness in this world." Through prayer, praise, and worship, we engage in spiritual warfare. It is not just about resisting evil forces; it's about standing firm in faith, using the tools God has provided to push back the enemy's advances. The Subconscious Mind, operating on the spiritual frequency of NOW faith, becomes a critical battleground. When we anchor ourselves in faith, we resist the lower vibrations of fear, doubt, and confusion that the enemy sends to disrupt our journey.

When you master these practices—praise, prayer, worship, and spiritual warfare - you will begin to experience the true power of thought and the dynamic laws that govern creation. Your life will transform as you attract success, abundance, and fulfillment through faith and conviction, allowing God's plans to manifest fully in your reality. They will serve as divine frequencies that help us align both the Conscious and Subconscious Minds with the will of God. Understanding how to use these spiritual tools enables us to fully embrace the power that God has already given us. We become attuned to the higher frequency of faith, allowing God's guidance to flow freely into our lives.

When you consistently engage in these practices, you safeguard your mind and spirit from the enemy's attempts to steal your blessings, just as the passage in Matthew 11:12 describes the Kingdom of Heaven being under siege. Each of these spiritual disciplines keeps you connected to the divine frequency where true success, abundance, and divine direction reside. The key lies in knowing how to maintain your connection to this higher realm, understanding that your thoughts shape the world around you, and that in faith, all things are possible.

FOUNDATIONAL SCRIPTURES AS THE KEYS TO THE KINGDOM

"As a man thinketh in his heart, so is he."
(Proverbs 23:7b KJV)

"...This, then is my condition: on my own I can serve God's laws only with my mind, while my human nature serves the law of sin." (Romans 7:26b GNT)

"Thanks be to God, who does this through our Lord Christ Jesus." (Romans 7:26a GNT)

"The person who was put right with God through faith shall live." "God's anger is revealed from heaven against all the sin and evil of the people whose evil ways prevent the truth from being known. God punishes them, because what can be known about God is plain to them, for God himself made it plain. Ever since God created the world, his invisible qualities, both his eternal power and his divine nature, have been clearly seen; they are perceived in the things that God has made. So those people have no excuse at all! They know God, but they do not give him the honor that belongs to him, nor do they thank him. Instead, their thoughts have become complete nonsense, and their empty minds are filled with darkness. They say they are wise, but they are fools; instead of worshiping the immortal God, they worship images made to look like mortals or birds or animals or reptiles. And so God has given those people over to do the filthy things their hearts desire, and they do shameful things with each other. They exchange the truth *about God for a lie; they worship and serve what God has created instead of the Creator himself, who is to be praised forever! Amen. Because they do this, God has given them over to shameful passions. Even the women pervert the natural use of their sex by unnatural acts."* (Prison culture embraces and re-enforces this disobedience). *"In the same way the men give up natural sexual relations with women and burn with passion for each other. Men do shameful things with each other, and as a result they bring upon themselves the punishment they deserve for their wrongdoing".* (The words: <u>men-who-have-sex-with-men</u> translate into two Greek words that refer to passive and active participation in homosexual acts). *"Because those people refuse to keep in mind the true knowledge about God, he has given them over to corrupted minds, so that they do the things that they should not do. They are filled with all kinds of wickedness, evil, greed, and vice; they are full of jealousy, murder, fighting, deceit, and malice. They gossip and speak evil of one another; they are hateful to God, insolent, proud, and boastful; they think of more ways to do evil; they dis-obey their parents; they have no conscience; they do not keep their promises, and they show no kindness or pity for others. They know that God's law says that people who live in this way deserve death. Yet, not only do they continue to do these very things, but they even approve of others who do them."* (Romans 1:17-32 GNT)

"THERE is therefore now no condemnation to those who are in Christ Jesus, who do not walk according to the flesh, but according to the Spirit. For the <u>Law of the Spirit of life in Christ Jesus</u> has made me free from the <u>Law of Sin and Death</u>. For what the Law could not do in that it was weak through the flesh, God did by sending His own Son in the likeness of sinful flesh (which in Hebrew is "sarx"), on account of sin: He condemned sin in the sarx, that the righteous requirement of the law might be fulfilled in us who do not walk according to the sarx but according to the Spirit. For those who live according to the sarx set their minds on the things of the sarx, but those who live according to the Spirit, the things of the Spirit. For to be sarx minded is death, but to be spiritually minded is life and peace. Because the sarx mind is enmity against God; for it is not subject

to the law of God, nor indeed can be. So then, those who are in the sarx can-
not please God. But you are not in the sarx but in the Spirit, if indeed the
Spirit of God dwells in you. Now if anyone does not have the Spirit of
Christ, he is not His. And if Christ is in you, the body is dead because of sin,
but the Spirit is life because of righteousness. But if the Spirit of Him who
raised Jesus from the dead dwells in you, He who raised Christ from the dead
will also give life to your mortal bodies through His Spirit who dwells in
you. Therefore, brethren, we are debtors—not to the sarx, to live according
to the sarx. For if you live according to the sarx you will die; but if by the
Spirit you put to death the deeds of the body, you will live. For as many as
are led by the Spirit of God, these are sons of God. For you did not receive
the spirit of bondage again to fear, but you received the Spirit of adoption
by whom we cry out, "Abba, Father." The Spirit Himself bears witness with
our spirit that we are children of God, and if children, then heirs—heirs of
God and joint heirs with Christ, if indeed we suffer with Him, that we may
also be glorified together. (Romans 8:1-17 NIV)

"Finally, my brethren, be strong in the Lord and in the power of His
might. Put on the whole armor of God, that you may be able to stand
against the wiles of the devil. For we do not wrestle against flesh and blood,
but against principalities, against powers, against the rulers of the darkness
of this age, against spiritual hosts of wickedness in the heavenly places.
Therefore take up the whole armor of God, that you may be able to with-
stand in the evil day, and having done all, to stand. Stand therefore, having
girded your waist with truth, having put on the breastplate of righteous-
ness, and having shod your feet with the preparation of the gospel of peace;
above all, taking the shield of faith with which you will be able to quench
all the fiery darts of the wicked one. And take the helmet of salvation,
and the sword of the Spirit, which is the word of God; praying always with
all prayer and supplication in the Spirit, being watchful to this end with all
perseverance and supplication for all the saints"
(Ephesians 6:10-18 NKJV)

CONTENTS

| 1 |

NOW Faith-Transform Thoughts
into Tangible Results

Tap into the foundational biblical principles of NOW Faith and thought to create rapid, life-changing results in every area of your life.

The foundation of all creation lies in the power of thought and NOW faith. To understand how reality is shaped, we must first recognize that nothing exists without purpose, intention, and divine order. This concept of divine thought is the origin of everything we see, touch, experience, and achieve. When we begin to grasp the significance of thought in the process of creation, we open the door to understanding how our thoughts, rooted in NOW faith, can align with God's eternal plan and manifest His promises into our lives.

Everything we see, touch, experience, and achieve begins with a divine thought. The world we live in was not the result of mere accident or a random cosmic event; it was birthed by intentional, intelligent design and divine will. From the words spoken in Genesis to the formation of every star in the heavens, everything that exists today originated in the perfect plan of God. As human beings created in His image, we have the ability to receive the images God reveals to us and, by holding fast to these visions, manifest His created matter into our reality through the power of thought. Yet, there is an inherent

1

distinction between idle thinking and purposeful, NOW faith-filled thought.

At the core of our ability to manifest change in our lives is the principle of NOW faith. As Hebrews 11:1 tells us, "Now faith is the substance of things hoped for, the evidence of things not seen." This passage reveals that faith is not just a passive belief in something abstract or distant. It is a dynamic and active force, creating substance out of hope, pulling unseen realities into the tangible world. *NOW faith* doesn't look to the future with uncertainty but claims promises in the present moment, believing that what is hoped for already exists in the spiritual realm.

To fully harness the power of thought, we must first understand its alignment with the spiritual laws God has put into place. From the beginning of time, we were given Authority, Dominion, And Might (ADAM) over the earth, not just in terms of physical control but in our ability to co-create with the divine. "And God said, Let us make man in our image, after our likeness: and let them have ADAM..." (Genesis 1:26). This ADAM extends to the power we have in our thoughts and words. What we think, and ultimately believe, shapes our reality in ways far more profound than most understand.

However, the Bible also provides cautionary wisdom regarding the misuse of this power. Proverbs 23:7 warns us, "For as he thinketh in his heart, so is he." This scripture reveals the undeniable truth that whatever is conceived in the heart—whether positive or negative—will manifest in a person's life. It is not enough to occasionally think a good thought. The condition of your heart, what you consistently meditate on, shapes who you are and what you will become. Therefore, one of the first principles of thought is stewardship. We must be vigilant, deliberate, and discerning in what we allow to take root in our hearts.

NOW faith is what transforms our thoughts from fleeting ideas into reality. Unlike simple belief, which often looks to the future, *NOW faith* is immediate, rooted in the conviction that what we believe already exists. It is faith in the present tense, an unwavering certainty that what God has promised is already in motion, even if it remains unseen to the physical eye. This concept of *NOW faith* is threaded throughout the Bible, with countless examples of individuals acting on faith in the moment, confident in God's promises even when circumstances suggested otherwise.

Consider Abraham, who, despite his old age and the barrenness of Sarah's womb, believed in God's promise to make him a father of nations. "He staggered not at the promise of God through unbelief; but was strong in faith, giving glory to God; and being fully persuaded that, what he had promised, he was able also to perform" (Romans 4:20-21 KJV). This kind of faith, rooted in the "now," activated the divine process that ultimately brought the promise to fruition. Abraham's example teaches us that *NOW faith* dismisses the limitations of the natural world and places full trust in the spiritual principles that govern creation.

One of the primary tools to attain the desires of our hearts is through the practice of meditation. Joshua 1:8 reminds us to keep the book of the law on our lips, meditating on it day and night so that we can act according to it and thus find success. In meditation, we affirm the book of the law, speaking God's promises into our subconscious minds with NOW faith and conviction. Through this process, we actively speak life into our circumstances, shaping the reality we wish to experience by allowing God's promises to penetrate deep within us.

When we meditate day and night, we are planting seeds of God's Word in the fertile garden of our hearts, and this practice yields varying results based on the faith we invest in the process. As outlined in the Parable of the Sower (Matthew 13), even the seeds that fall on good soil produce crops in different measures—some yielding 100 times, some 60, and others 30. This difference is a reflection of how much faith one has in the growth process. A man with 30-fold NOW faith works only 30% of the time, doubting and hesitating 70% of the time. Meanwhile, the 100-fold man operates in NOW faith continuously, nurturing the seed of God's Word through meditation without wavering or allowing doubt to take root. He is like the tree planted by streams of water, which bears fruit in season and prospers in all he does (Psalm 1:2-3).

The stronger the faith, the greater the harvest. When we meditate on God's Word and speak His promises day and night, we operate on the frequency of faith, and the seed that we plant in our hearts will yield accordingly. The hundredfold return is the result of unwavering NOW faith, constantly nurturing the seeds with God's promises.

But just as a farmer faces weeds in his field, we too encounter "weeds" of doubt and fear that attempt to choke the harvest. These weeds are sown by the unseen spiritual enemy while we are unaware, and they are designed to project negative thoughts into the fertile soil of our subconscious mind. Jesus spoke of this in another parable: "The Kingdom of Heaven is like a man who sowed good seed in his field. But while everyone was sleeping, his enemy came and sowed weeds among the wheat and went away" (Matthew 13:24-25). If we fail to meditate day and night on God's promises and grow lax in our faith, we give the enemy the opportunity to plant doubt, fear, and limitation in the soil of our minds.

Thus, it is crucial to remain vigilant in faith, constantly feeding the Positive Throne of ADAM within us by affirming God's promises. By removing all negative strongholds from the subconscious mind and installing in their stead our Positive Throne of ADAM, we align ourselves with the path of attainment and happiness. The positive thoughts that align with God's promises will overwrite the negative strongholds and dissipate their power. As long as we keep our faith active, those strongholds will have no power over us.

To truly flourish, we must speak life into our circumstances, water our seeds through consistent meditation, and rest in the assurance that God's dynamic laws of creation are at work. Our role is to trust that the process is in motion and to cultivate a mindset that reflects this trust. When we understand the importance of NOW faith, consistent meditation, and positive affirmations aligned with God's Word, we unlock the full potential of the Authority, Dominion, And Might (ADAM) that God has given us since the beginning.

As we delve deeper, the next step is to understand how the principles of faith and thought are processed in the human mind. There are two realms of thinking that govern every aspect of life: the Conscious Mind, seated in the brain of the human skull, and the Subconscious Mind, which operates from the brain of the human heart. Each mind functions on a distinct frequency, much like the difference between AM and FM radio transmissions. Understanding these frequencies will unlock the deeper dynamics of NOW faith, meditation, and manifestation.

| 2 |

Demolish Stronghold Mindsets That Sabotage Success

*U*ncover and dismantle the limiting thought patterns and beliefs planted *by the enemy and life's hardships, allowing you to align with God's truth and reclaim your path to abundance.*

Have you ever felt trapped in a cycle of self-doubt and fear, where your dreams seem perpetually out of reach? Are you ready to confront the invisible barriers that hold you back from experiencing the abundance that God promises? In this chapter, we will uncover and dismantle the limiting thought patterns and beliefs that life's hardships as well as the enemy has planted deep within you. With the guiding wisdom of Scripture—*"For though we walk in the flesh, we do not war after the flesh: (For the weapons of our warfare are not carnal, but mighty through God by the pulling down of strongholds)"* (II Corinthians 10:3-4 KJV)—we will arm ourselves with divine truths to reclaim our paths to success and fulfillment.

The Wonderful Counselor is responsive to thought. He creates for us what we project into His Spirit during prayer and meditation. This projection is activated only through the frequency of the Subconscious Mind. The reason our conscious desires do not always manifest in reality is twofold: One, we are not projecting our thoughts with enough conviction to activate the frequency of the Subconscious Mind. Or two, there are strongholds created by fear, dread, superstition, and doubt in the Subconscious Mind that cause our thinking to wander fearfully astray. These strongholds are enemy-planted weed seeds of the Conscious Mind, buried in the Subconscious due to stronger convictions that have long been forgotten. They are primarily born of painful experiences and thus primarily negative—attracting and creating lack, limitation, disease, destruction, death, unhappiness, and constant unguided movement and actions.

Recognizing these strongholds is the first step toward liberation. They often masquerade as protective thoughts, whispering that they are keeping you safe when, in fact, they are stifling your potential. You may find yourself thinking, "I'm not good enough," "Success is for others, not me," or "I'll never overcome this challenge." Each of these thoughts feeds the strongholds, fortifying the walls that keep you from stepping into the abundant life God has planned for you. In this chapter, we will identify the root causes of these negative thought patterns and provide you with practical tools to pull down and dismantle them, paving the way for a mind renewed in Christ.

Imagine what it would feel like to break free from the chains of your past and the lies that have held you captive. To walk confidently in the truth of who you are and the dreams God has placed within you. As we journey together through the powerful dynamic laws, strategies, and spiritual truths in this chapter, you will learn how to uproot those harmful beliefs, replacing them with declarations of faith that resonate with God's promises. By actively engaging in this transformative process, you'll find that the very obstacles that once stood in your way can become steppingstones toward your greatest successes.

Get ready to reclaim the untapped power of your Subconscious Mind and unleash this 24-hour memory machine to bring to you all that you have set your thoughts to do. Within man is a mind that never sleeps, that is constantly active, with untold reservoirs that have never yet been plumbed—a mind of such infinite capacity and power that it could not possibly belong to one man alone. "Let this mind be in you, which was also in Christ Jesus" *(Philippians 2:5).* The Subconscious Mind of Christ that He gives freely to man is all-powerful, generous, and selfless.

The memory of the Subconscious Mind is perfect—not just for important facts but for every shade, detail, and scene ever experienced. A skilled psychiatrist can run back twenty years in a patient's Subconscious, eliciting a scene from when the patient was six years old, and lo, the scene unfolds in color, sound, and detail. Those memories are all there, recorded as vividly as a digital smartphone picture or a TikTok video. The background sounds of the cicada filling the Mississippi summer air, the horse ranch smell of clean shavings, dewy alfalfa, pungent thrush, burning hair, or Pepi Coat Conditioner, the NYC sounds of nonstop honking horns, the grimace of a countenance, the movement of a person, words and inflections—all exact, even to the emotional impact. Yet, this is a scene the Conscious Mind may cnever even noticed or has long forgotten the event altogether.

The probing of the Subconscious Mind has unearthed a vast store of unknown material. Under deep hypnosis, patients who suffered various traumas have described noises and surroundings that could only have been experienced in the womb. Similarly, others have described vivid scenes and times in crystal clear detail that would have been impossible for them to know or witness. The Subconscious Mind is the most powerful creative instrument in the universe; it spans space and time, manifests thought frequency and words into form, Matter and substance, reaches out to all knowledge, and exists as the great equalizer within every man, woman, and child.

The delicate Conscious Mind, though it remembers only fragments of years and holds a handful of facts, grasps the basic principles of thought but struggles to navigate its immediate environment. Yet, it carries immense significance as it stands as the master of our mental realm, while the formidable Subconscious Mind acts as its faithful servant. The Subconscious dutifully follows every command from the Conscious Mind—without hesitation or doubt. This dynamic reveals both the challenge and the opportunity before you; the key lies in how well you harness and direct this powerful relationship.

No one consciously desires to be sick, impoverished, imprisoned, unloved, or unsuccessful. It would be impossible to find anyone in the world who admits to consciously wanting these negative things. Yet, if they have them, just as surely as there are the dynamics of life, they have ordered them for themselves.

The individual is often a victim of Strongholds set into the Subconscious Mind through the gateway of the Conscious Mind. These strongholds lie hidden deep within, akin to a forgetful dog burying a bone, oblivious to both the location of its hiding spot and the act of burying it altogether. These Strongholds within the Subconscious Mind are responsible for the great masses of unfulfilled people—those who flock to psychiatrists, searching for answers. These strongholds spread more dysfunction in individual lives than any other single thing. Strongholds have given the world insecurity, hostility, greed, corruption, and hate. They have cast both individuals and families out of alignment with God's guidance.

Consider, for instance, the stronghold of poverty, which can arise from seemingly innocuous phrases sown in our subconscious during childhood. Expressions like "I'm not made out of money," "Money doesn't grow on trees," "It takes money to make money," or "There's not enough money to go around" take root in the fertile soil of our minds. Reflect on this: the Subconscious Mind starts to internalize a belief in scarcity, convinced that resources are finite. A child may find it impossible to request and enjoy a simple treat from the ice cream truck, as their family's mindset revolves around the notion of insufficient funds. Consequently, the cycle of lack and limitation becomes a self-fulfilling prophecy, defining the very fabric of their existence.

A sick man yearns for healing, yet his condition endures, revealing a deep-rooted stronghold within. The Subconscious Mind often clings to phrases like, "You'd better put on a coat, or you'll catch pneumonia and die," "Diabetes and high blood pressure run in my family," or "There are countless new strains of COVID-19 in my state." To make matters worse, it absorbs the flood of daily messages from pharmaceutical ads, presenting ordinary discomforts as indicators of severe ailments that can only be alleviated by a pill—sometimes even one that poses serious risks to life. With such powerful subconscious strongholds in place, how can one genuinely aspire to health?

A lonely soul longs for love and connection, yet no matter the situation, they find it impossible to draw in a partner or cultivate a circle of friends. A stronghold may lie beneath the surface, repelling affection with thoughts like, "Nobody ever did anything for me," "I can do bad all by myself," or "People just want to use you." To compound the issue, a stronghold can breed feelings of unworthiness: "You're not good enough," "You don't amount to anything," or "Nobody loves you." The Subconscious Mind might even whisper, "How could anyone truly love me when I'm nothing? They must be nothing too." The truth is, the Subconscious Mind is a formidable force—it brings these beliefs to life, transforming the negative thoughts into tangible reality, sometimes easier that the intentional positive desires.

Who can be successful with a subconscious stronghold constantly convincing them that everyone else is better? Who could achieve anything if they are convinced that achievement is meaningless? Who can rise to great heights if they believe they have no capability? Or if they are held back by the belief that their past disqualifies them from a good future? The answer is no one. For the Subconscious Mind is a great creator—it creates exactly what is projected into it by your acceptance of the image revealed. It creates according to what it receives from the Conscious Mind.

We can, however, remove these strongholds. By understanding the Laws and Dynamics of Life, you can dismantle the causes of these strongholds so they will plague you no more. Nothing is impossible. The Conscious Mind controls the Subconscious Mind, and when the Subconscious Mind is aligned with the Mind of Christ, it becomes all-powerful on Earth and throughout the universe. Every condition, circumstance, and manifestation in your life can be changed to suit your conscious desires.

Christ's resurrection canceled every stronghold, including the greatest one—the fear of death. *"He is not here, for he is risen."* (Matthew 28:6). Through His victory, Christ brought hope and salvation to all who put their trust in Him. That triumph placed Him at the right hand of God on His throne. It is this yoke-destroying, stronghold-casting, throne of authority He shares with us as we take our place as His body. This is the positive throne of Authority, Dominion, and Might (ADAM), which we now possess.

By removing all negative strongholds from the Subconscious Mind and installing in their place our Positive Throne of ADAM, we are led on a path of attainment and happiness. There is no need for a special process to remove these negative strongholds—simply turning on the Law of Life in Christ Jesus will overwrite the negative with the positive. This Positive Throne of ADAM automatically installs in the Subconscious Mind, displacing the strongholds. The existence of this positive throne within will dissipate all negative strongholds, allowing the individual to expand to the full blossom of his or her power.

For instance, if you find yourself frequently battling illness, there's no need to delve into the depths of your Subconscious Mind to uncover the stronghold responsible for your sickness. Instead, it's far more impactful to establish your new Positive Throne of ADAM. This throne boldly proclaims, "It is natural to be well; health and vitality are inherent birthrights of humanity. You exist within a perfect spiritual body, and your physical form, as an expression of this flawless spiritual essence, is perfect as well." Once your Positive Throne of ADAM is firmly established in the Subconscious Mind, the negative "sickness stronghold" will begin to wither away. This formidable Positive Throne of ADAM draws its power from the incorruptible seeds found within the covenant promises of salvation and rebirth as revealed in the Bible. However, this potent source of Authority, Dominion, and Might can only be activated when the believer fully embraces these promises as truth, demonstrating unwavering conviction. In doing so, they inherently pull down the negative strongholds, which are ultimately nothing but deceptive lies.

The Conscious Realm operates through our physical senses: touch, taste, smell, hearing, and sight. This RAM memory serves as the processing hub for incoming data, evaluating the presence of strongholds and determining whether to retain the memory for immediate use or discard it as extraneous. Every thought must first be navigated in this realm before being transferred to the Subconscious Mind for permanent storage. Each thought is categorized as either useful or unnecessary, yet every impression is meticulously recorded. Negative strongholds are etched in this space, and unseen spiritual forces exploit them to disrupt a person's thought processes, leading to instability and confusion.

As a human being, you will make mistakes in arriving at truth. Do not allow remorse to become a stronghold. Be joyful that error has disclosed truth. Confess your sins, and God, who is faithful, will forgive you and cleanse you of all unrighteousness. That's the end of the transaction. It's over. You only have the dynamic effect that the cause set into motion to deal with, but the transgression is squashed. You must not linger in remorse even a moment beyond confession. Imagine the tragedy of a person trudging through life, weighed down by self-blame for every misstep, letting discouragement and shame become constant companions. This self-inflicted burden becomes a fertile ground for strongholds to take root in the Subconscious Mind, anchoring pain and regret instead of freedom and grace. Let us not be afraid of making a mistake or of suffering the consequence if the mistake is made. Just be sure to get the lesson from the mistake, that way you only have to suffer the consequence of each mistake only once and no more. When you have a desire, allow it to unfold in its own time. Don't confuse your Subconscious Mind by constantly saying, "Go; wait; go; stop," wearing it down with indecision. This wavering back and forth burdens you with the weight of uncertainty, leaving you unstable in every area of your life. This isn't about delving into the depths of our subconscious to unearth every negative seed; it's about flooding our minds with the glory light of truth in God's promises.

Our minds function within two distinct realms: the conscious and the subconscious. The Conscious Mind acts as our immediate navigator, processing sensory information and helping us manage the tasks of daily life. Yet, beneath this surface lies the Subconscious Mind, rooted within the heart, where the true issues of life take shape and resonate on a spiritual frequency beyond our senses. This is the space where negative strongholds may dwell—but it is also the fertile ground for establishing the Positive Throne of ADAM, if we consciously choose to plant it. Now, let us explore the pathway to fully unlocking this divine potential within.

Strongholds are those invisible, yet powerful, mental fortresses we construct over time, often built upon lies and deceptions we've unwittingly accepted as truth. These strongholds warp our perception of reality and obstruct the divine flow of blessings into our lives. They manifest as recurring obstacles, negative thought patterns, or habitual cycles of defeat that seem inescapable. The first step to dismantling them is to acknowledge their existence. You must look within and recognize these negative patterns for what they are: indicators of deep-seated strongholds. Only when you see them for what they are, can you begin the process of breaking free.

Once you've identified these strongholds, the work of renewal begins. The Word of God is the only truth powerful enough to overwrite the lies that have rooted themselves in your subconscious. Romans 12:2 reminds us to *"be transformed by the renewing of your mind."* Immerse yourself in Scripture, let the truths of God's promises soak into your soul, and allow the Mind of Christ to take residence where deception once reigned. As you feed on this truth, your mind is being renewed, layer by layer, reshaping your perception and aligning it with God's design for your life. This is no passive activity; it's a deliberate and active reprogramming of the thought patterns that persist on holding you captive.

But renewing your mind is only part of the process—your words hold tremendous creative power. Speak life over yourself. Declare God's promises, vocalize His truth with authority, for what you speak reinforces your beliefs in the Subconscious Mind. Let your words be an affirmation of your identity in Christ—health, prosperity, love, and success are your birthrights. Cultivate gratitude in this process. A thankful heart raises your spiritual frequency, attracting more reasons to be grateful.

Finally, install the Positive Throne of ADAM by consistently affirming who you are in Christ. Each day, reinforce the truth of who you are—royalty, blessed and favored, walking in divine authority. As you do this, the strongholds of the past will crumble, and the Dynamic Law of Attraction will begin to operate in your life, drawing the abundance and success that are yours by divine right. In the appendix of this book, I have transferred the words of God's promises into powerful confessions that are proven prepare the field of the heart to pull down strongholds.

Remember, the Subconscious Mind creates according to what the Conscious Mind commands. By feeding it with God's truth, we align ourselves with His divine will, unlocking the path to spiritual freedom. Let us not be held captive by unseen forces using old strongholds against us. Instead, let's step into the authority we've been given, breaking every chain, and walking boldly into the abundant life God has ordained for us.

| 3 |

Employ Violent Faith: Take Back Our Kingdom Rights

*Y*ou've been given the keys to Heaven's authority—now learn to wield them, violently reclaiming what's yours and binding on earth what's bound in Heaven by the guarding of your thoughts, ideas, and words, with assured power and duty as a Kingdom citizen

Whatever has been stolen must be restored if we are to prove ourselves faithful stewards over the manifested Matter in our lives. In the unseen realms, there are marauders—shadowy figures influenced by evil spirits—whose sole objective is to plunder the Kingdom of Heaven. These raiders are cunning, relentless, and highly attuned to the faintest vibrations of doubt, fear, and hesitation. They lurk at the threshold of God's people's prayers, waiting for the precise moment when the words of faith, planted in the fertile soil of the spirit, are negated by seeds of doubt.

These forces are not mere human beings, but powers, and principalities, dark spirits that manipulate those they control, driving them to seize the blessings and revelations that belong to God's chosen ones. Every prayer uttered in faith sets in motion the manifestation of divine promises. The Holy Spirit brings forth images, inspiration, and strategies from the heart of God through the Mind of Christ. But just as swiftly as these blessings begin to take form, the evil forces come to snatch them away—when God's people waver.

These raiders, both spiritual and physical, are fueled by the words of doubt, fear, and disbelief that God's people so often release when confronted with adversity. They are patient, for they know that every blessing, every breakthrough, every revelation from Heaven can be undermined when doubt creeps into the heart of a believer.

Picture this: a man of God has prayed for financial breakthrough. The Wonderful Counselor has given him a clear visual image of abundance, a path laid before him in divine wisdom. His words, once filled with NOW faith, have already set the wheels of manifestation into motion. But as time passes, without the immediate evidence of that breakthrough, fear begins to whisper. "What if it doesn't happen?" "Maybe it wasn't God's will after all." And then, the fatal words escape his lips: "I don't know if this is going to work."

In that moment, the spiritual raiders swoop in. The prayer that had been rising to Heaven on wings of faith is now weighed down by the chains of doubt. The blessing, once in his grasp, begins to slip away. What the man of God doesn't realize is that those blessings are still hovering in the spiritual realm, waiting to be claimed—but abandoned the moment his words reversed what his faith once declared.

The dark forces, influenced by ancient spirits of the old ones rejoice in these moments of hesitation. They feast upon the uncertainty of God's people, stealing the abandoned blessings that should have manifested to them in the physical realm. They take what was once intended for God's people and twist it for their own purposes, redirecting the spoils of the Kingdom into the hands of those who do not honor God, who mock Him, and who repurpose His gifts for evil.

Think of the artist who once prayed for inspiration, the musician who sought divine creativity, or the entrepreneur who asked for wisdom to build a business that honors God. Each received their answer in the form of an image, a divine download from the Wonderful Counselor. Yet, when doubt whispered, "You're not talented enough," or "This dream is too big for you," or "Why would God help you succeed?"—their prayers began to unravel. The very moment they spoke those words of doubt, the blessings, like vapor, slipped from their grasp.

It is in these moments that the raiders strike. These blessings, discarded by those who once prayed for them, are eagerly claimed by others—those who have no connection to the Kingdom, yet understand the power of words and thoughts in ways that even many believers do not. They take what was once a divine idea, intended to advance God's Kingdom, and twist it for worldly gain.

"You believe that God is one; you do well [to believe that]. The demons also believe [that], and shudder and bristle [in awe-filled terror—they have seen His wrath]!" (James 2:19 AMP)

The result is clear. We see it in the books that teach the principles of success without honoring the Author of life. We hear it in the music that inspires but lacks the reverence for the true Source of all creativity. We watch it play out in movies that captivate audiences with stories that echo divine truths, yet never give credit to the Creator.

The raiders have become masters at this art—seizing what was once meant for God's people and turning it into worldly success devoid of spiritual substance. Their influence can be seen in every sphere of society, from entertainment to business, from politics to education. They have perfected the craft of taking divine revelation and repackaging it as something secular, something devoid of the honor and glory due to God.

But here lies the greater tragedy: many of God's people, blinded by their own doubt, walk away from these blessings, leaving them abandoned on the battlefield of faith. They speak words of fear, canceling out the very prayers they once spoke with conviction. The enemy, always waiting in the shadows, is quick to collect these forsaken blessings and use them to build empires that mock the Kingdom of Heaven.

There is an ancient law maxim that states, *"The winner is the last man standing on the battlefield."* It is not the one who fought the hardest or who had the most skill, but the one who endured, who remained steadfast, and refused to retreat in the face of adversity. This law maxim applies not only in physical battles but also in the spiritual warfare that surrounds us daily. The raiders of the Kingdom of Heaven wait for God's people to abandon the battlefield of faith, knowing full well that blessings are claimed by those who stand their ground until the very end.

On the battlefield of prayer and manifestation, the spiritual forces of darkness circle, waiting for the moment when believers give in to doubt and fear, leaving the ground they once fought for. They swoop in, not because they have won the battle, but because the believer has walked away from the blessing they had prayed for. It is in the final moments, just before the breakthrough, that the enemy works the hardest to convince God's people to leave the battlefield. But those who stand firm, who refuse to speak words of doubt, who cling to their faith in the Wonderful Counselor, will be the last ones standing—and it is they who will claim the victory, seizing what the enemy sought to steal.

Stay on the battlefield of faith, for the blessings are yours to claim, and the only way to lose is to leave before the victory is manifested. Victory is not given to the faint-hearted or the doubtful but to those who remain, enduring the trials, the waiting, and the temptations to give up. When you stand firm in your NOW faith, you ensure that the enemy's hands are empty, for only those who endure to the end inherit the Kingdom.

This is the clarion call to every believer—take back the Kingdom of Heaven. Recognize the power of your words, for the forces of darkness are attuned to them just as much as the angels of Heaven. Do not let fear or doubt rob you of the blessings God has prepared for you. Do not abandon your prayers when the manifestation is near. Guard your words, protect your faith, and stand firm in the promises of God.

The enemy is waiting, lurking for the moment you give up, the moment you allow doubt to sever the connection to the manifestation. But the Wonderful Counselor has already begun the work. He has shown you the image, the vision, the path. Do not be swayed. For every word of faith released in NOW faith will always attract the Kingdom's resources. Stay the course, and what God has set in motion will come to pass.

Take back the Kingdom. Claim what is rightfully yours. Guard your thoughts, guard your words, and let no spirit of fear or doubt steal what has been prepared for you. Let the raiders of Heaven's treasures be defeated, and let the blessings of God's people manifest in all their fullness. The Kingdom of Heaven is yours to claim—take it with force, with faith, and with unwavering trust in the One who has called you.

"From the days of John the Baptist until now, the Kingdom of heaven has been subject to violence, and the violent people have been raiding it."
(Matthew 11:12 NIV)

"And I will give unto thee the keys of the Kingdom of heaven: whatso-
ever thou shall bind on earth shall be bound in heaven: and whatsoever thou
shall loose on earth shall be loosed in heaven." (Matthew 16: 19. KJV)

For centuries, the greatest stories, the most awe-inspiring music, and the most profound ideas have shaped our world. These creations have moved hearts, stirred imaginations, and driven people toward extraordinary feats. But as we look closer at the origins of such inspired works, we begin to see that many of them bear the unmistakable fingerprints of divine wisdom—a wisdom that has been systematically raided by those who have refused to acknowledge the source. These works, born from the ideas and revelations of the Kingdom of Heaven, have been seized and repackaged without giving credit to the One who spoke the first word of creation into existence.

The Story of George Washington Carver:

George Washington Carver, a man of immense faith and unparalleled ingenuity, carried a simple Bible and a humble peanut into his laboratory, and from those two sources alone, he unraveled the mysteries of nature. Carver wasn't a scientist driven by ambition or worldly recognition; he was a man moved by his deep connection with God. In every experiment, in every new discovery, Carver sought the wisdom of the Creator, trusting in divine guidance more than any textbook or human knowledge. His laboratory became a sacred space where he communed with the Wonderful Counselor, praying for revelation, and waiting in stillness for the answers to unfold.

Carver's reverence for God, and his unwavering belief that all wisdom originates from the Almighty, led him to invent over 300 products derived from the peanut alone, including adhesives, dyes, paints, plastics, gasoline, and even medicinal products. Beyond peanuts, his discoveries extended into sweet potatoes, soybeans, and clay, impacting industries as diverse as agriculture, textiles, and medicine. His breakthroughs laid the groundwork for much of modern agriculture and manufacturing, yet Carver never sought glory for himself. He attributed every discovery, every flash of insight, to the hand of God, believing that the Creator had hidden the mysteries of the universe in the simplest of creations—waiting for a heart humble enough to ask for them.

But for all his humility, for all the wonders that passed through his hands, the world did not always treat Carver with the honor and recognition he deserved. Many of his inventions were stolen, the credit given to others who did not acknowledge the source of their wisdom. These individuals, driven by greed and worldly ambition, raided the Kingdom of Heaven without giving glory to the One from whom all knowledge flows. They took Carver's innovations and marketed them under their own names, reaping the financial rewards and societal accolades that should have belonged to the man who had discovered them in quiet communion with God.

Carver did not fight for recognition, nor seek fame or wealth; he sought only to serve, to uplift his people, and to honor God with the gifts he had been given. Yet, in the shadows, men and corporations capitalized on his genius, exploiting his discoveries without so much as a thank-you to the Creator who had inspired them. History is riddled with examples of Carver's inventions being attributed to others, many of whom had no intention of acknowledging the divine inspiration behind them.

Perhaps the most egregious injustice was not merely the theft of Carver's intellectual property, but the erasure of the spirit with which he approached his work. For Carver, every experiment was an act of worship. Every discovery was a testament to the glory of God, a confirmation of the wisdom hidden in creation, waiting to be uncovered by those willing to listen to the still, small voice. Yet, when others took his work, they stripped it of this sacred context, reducing it to mere products, mere tools for profit and power.

Carver's story is a reminder of the raiders of the Kingdom—those who steal divine revelation without honoring the Source. Like many others who have sought God's wisdom, Carver's revelations were plundered by those who did not acknowledge the hand of God in their success. They took the fruits of his labor and used them for worldly gain, leaving the man who had knelt in prayer and communion with his Bible and his peanut largely forgotten by the very industries he revolutionized.

Yet, Carver's legacy endures—not because of the patents he did or did not receive, or the wealth he never amassed, but because of his unwavering commitment to honoring God with his life's work. His story reminds us that true wisdom comes from above, and those who seek it with pure hearts will find it. The world may steal the credit, but it cannot steal the truth. Carver's innovations, inspired by the Holy Spirit, continue to impact the world today, even if the world has forgotten where they truly came from.

George Washington Carver stands as a testament to what is possible when a person seeks the wisdom of God above all else. His life is a reminder that the greatest discoveries, the most profound innovations, do not come from man's intellect alone but from a heart attuned to the frequencies of Heaven. And though his work was raided by those who refused to give credit where it was due, Carver's quiet, faithful pursuit of divine wisdom has left an indelible mark on history. He may not have received the recognition he deserved in his lifetime, but in the annals of the Kingdom of Heaven, his name is written among the greatest of God's stewards.

The Story of Nikola Tesla:

Nikola Tesla, a man whose mind was as electrifying as the very currents he sought to harness, was one of the greatest inventors the world has ever seen. His vision stretched far beyond the horizons of his time, and in many ways, beyond what we can still fully grasp today. Tesla wasn't merely interested in the physical act of invention; he was on a quest to unlock the secrets of the universe, to tap into the invisible forces that govern the world, and use them for the betterment of humanity. He believed in a world where free energy could be provided to all, where technology served as an equalizing force for good, and where power—literally and figuratively—was not something to be hoarded, but freely shared.

Yet, for all of his genius, Tesla's life became a dark testament to how those with selfish intent can raid the treasures of visionaries who, like him, were ahead of their time. Tesla's innovations in electricity, wireless transmission, radio waves, and even his early work in robotics, laid the groundwork for much of the technology that fuels modern life. But few know just how much was taken from him and how much of his work was exploited by others who sought profit and control rather than the greater good.

Tesla's story is one of visionary brilliance being plundered by those driven by greed, manipulation, and worldly power. Throughout his life, his groundbreaking discoveries were continuously sabotaged, stolen, and credited to others. Thomas Edison, for example, a contemporary and rival, is often praised as the father of electricity, yet it was Tesla's alternating current (AC) system that powered the modern world and became the standard for electrical distribution. Despite this, Tesla's AC work was opposed, challenged, and raided by Edison, who promoted his own, far less efficient, direct current (DC) system, not out of scientific integrity but to protect his financial investments.

Edison would go so far as to stage public demonstrations in which animals were electrocuted using AC in a cruel attempt to paint Tesla's innovations as dangerous.

But perhaps the most egregious theft of Tesla's brilliance came from J.P. Morgan, one of the most powerful financiers of the time. Tesla had envisioned a world where wireless power could be transmitted across vast distances. He built the Wardenclyffe Tower on Long Island, a massive structure designed to transmit free electricity wirelessly to the world, a project Tesla believed could uplift all of humanity. But when Morgan, who had originally funded Tesla's vision, realized that Tesla's technology could not be monetized—could not be metered and controlled for profit—he immediately withdrew his support, leaving Tesla's project to collapse. Not only did Morgan cut Tesla off financially, but he also blacklisted him, ensuring that no other investors would fund his work. Tesla's dream of free energy for all was raided by the greed of men who had no desire to see power, in any form, be given freely to the masses.

As Tesla's fortunes dwindled, so did the recognition of his name. Many of his later inventions, including early concepts for wireless communication, radar, and even the precursors to modern robotics, were either uncredited to him or actively suppressed. The world's most powerful forces—the very ones Tesla sought to transcend with his work—had raided the Kingdom of Heaven's secrets that Tesla had tapped into, and they twisted them for their own ends. Tesla, in his final years, died penniless and forgotten, a man whose ideas were raided, distorted, and used by others for selfish gain.

Even after his death, the raid continued. When Tesla died in 1943 in a New York hotel room, the FBI immediately seized all of his papers and notes. The government feared that Tesla's final, unpublished ideas—particularly those regarding wireless energy and his so-called "death ray"—would fall into enemy hands. To this day, much of Tesla's work remains classified or lost, hidden from public view. What was taken, and what has been used, remains a mystery to many.

Tesla's inventions could have revolutionized the world in ways that are hard to fathom. He was a man who believed that the secrets of the universe were to be shared, not hoarded. He believed in harnessing the invisible forces of nature, of tapping into the ether—the very fabric of the cosmos—for the betterment of all mankind. He did not seek wealth, fame, or control. He sought truth, and through that truth, he sought to free humanity from the physical limitations of energy and power. Yet, like the Kingdom of Heaven, Tesla's discoveries were raided by those who could see no further than their own ambitions.

The story of Nikola Tesla serves as a warning for what God calls "the just". There are unseen forces—spiritual and otherwise—that work tirelessly to steal the blessings of visionaries, those who receive divine wisdom and knowledge. These raiders of the Kingdom seek to plunder not for the betterment of humanity, but for the enrichment of themselves. They are driven by greed, fear, and the need to control. Just as Tesla's inventions were stolen, manipulated, and used for the gain of a few, so too are the blessings and prayers of God's people often intercepted by the spiritual raiders who whisper doubt and fear, causing many to walk away from their blessings.

Tesla's life is a reminder that the battlefield is not always visible. It is fought in the realms of thought, innovation, and divine inspiration. And just as in the Kingdom of Heaven, it is often the last one standing—the one who refuses to surrender to doubt, fear, and greed—who will ultimately claim the victory. Tesla may not have seen the full fruition of his work in his lifetime, but his ideas live on, echoing across time, a testament to the eternal nature of true wisdom.

Elon Musk, the visionary entrepreneur behind Tesla, Inc., has openly acknowledged his deep admiration for Nikola Tesla and his groundbreaking innovations. Musk's decision to name his electric car company "Tesla" was more than just a nod to the inventor's contributions to the world of electricity. It was a tribute to the man whose ideas were not only ahead of his time but whose approach to energy, invention, and innovation mirrored Musk's own ambitions. In many ways, Nikola Tesla's life and work profoundly influenced Musk's vision for the future—a future powered by renewable energy, technology, and an unwavering belief in the power of human ingenuity. And one that could be taken, as its uses have long been forfeited and walked away from.

Throughout history, many men and women of faith have drawn inspiration from their connection with God to develop groundbreaking ideas, innovations, and creations. However, many of these "heavenly downloads" have been stolen or suppressed, and the credit for their work has been wrongfully claimed by others. Here are a few notable examples of innovative men of God whose contributions were often overshadowed or taken by those with less honorable intentions:

1. Johann Gutenberg (1400-1468) – The Printing Press
Johann Gutenberg, a devout Christian, is widely credited with inventing the printing press around 1440, revolutionizing the dissemination of knowledge and making the Bible widely available to ordinary people. His invention is often recognized as one of the greatest technological advancements in history, significantly contributing to the spread of the Reformation and the distribution of religious texts.

However, while Gutenberg made history with his invention, he struggled financially and was embroiled in legal disputes that allowed others to profit from his work. His partner, Johann Fust, took control of Gutenberg's printing workshop after a legal disagreement, and Fust and Peter Schoffer (another printer) printed a Bible that many believed for years was Gutenberg's creation. Gutenberg's role was initially downplayed, and he received little financial reward or recognition for his contribution during his lifetime.

2. Isaac Newton (1643-1727) – Gravity and Faith

Isaac Newton, considered one of the greatest scientists of all time, was also a devout believer in God and saw his scientific work as a way to understand God's creation. His discovery of the laws of gravity and motion fundamentally changed our understanding of the universe, and he was instrumental in laying the groundwork for classical physics.

Despite his contributions to science, much of Newton's religious writing and his views on God's role in the universe were kept hidden for centuries. Newton's work on theology was often dismissed or ignored by later generations of secular scientists, who wanted to distance his scientific brilliance from his devout Christian faith. In many academic circles, his scientific legacy was separated from his belief in God, and the depth of his faith was largely concealed or minimized.

3. Michael Faraday (1791-1867) – Electromagnetism and Faith

Michael Faraday, one of the greatest experimental scientists of the 19th century, made foundational contributions to electromagnetism and electrochemistry. Faraday was deeply religious and belonged to the Sandemanian Church, a small Christian sect that greatly influenced his worldview and work. He saw his scientific discoveries as a way to illuminate God's laws in nature.

Despite his groundbreaking work, Faraday was often overshadowed by more prominent figures of his time. Many secular historians downplayed the role of his faith in his scientific work, and the connection between his devotion to God and his scientific achievements was not always acknowledged. His deep spiritual convictions were, in some ways, seen as an oddity by the scientific community, and his contributions were often credited solely to his experimental rigor, ignoring his belief that his insights were gifts from God.

4. Rudolf Diesel (1858-1913) – The Diesel Engine

Rudolf Diesel, the inventor of the diesel engine, was a man of Christian faith who believed in the betterment of society through technology. Diesel's invention of the high-efficiency engine revolutionized transportation and industry, and he believed that his work was inspired by God's call to improve the lives of the common man.

Unfortunately, Diesel's life ended mysteriously, and many of his ideas were stolen or appropriated by others after his death. His work was taken by corporate entities that commercialized his engine without giving him the proper recognition or compensation for his revolutionary invention. There are theories that his death may have been the result of foul play, as powerful industrialists sought to control and profit from his invention without his involvement.

5. Galileo Galilei (1564-1642) – Astronomy and Faith

Galileo Galilei, known as the "father of modern science," was a devout Catholic who believed that science and faith could coexist. He famously championed the heliocentric model of the solar system, which placed the sun, rather than the earth, at the center of the universe. Galileo's discoveries in astronomy and physics helped shape the scientific revolution.

However, Galileo's support for the heliocentric model brought him into direct conflict with the Catholic Church, which saw his work as heretical at the time. Although he remained a man of faith, Galileo was persecuted for his views, and the credit for his contributions was suppressed by the Church for many years. His works were censored, and he was placed under house arrest, limiting his ability to continue his research. Although he was eventually vindicated by history, the delay in recognizing his contributions was due to the raiding of his ideas by those who did not honor the source of his wisdom.

6. James Clerk Maxwell (1831-1879) – Electromagnetic Theory and Christian Faith

James Clerk Maxwell, one of the most important physicists in history, formulated the classical theory of electromagnetic radiation. Maxwell, a devout Christian, saw his work as an exploration of the order and laws that God had written into creation. His equations unified electricity, magnetism, and optics into a single theoretical framework, profoundly influencing modern physics.

Despite his monumental achievements, Maxwell's Christian faith was often overlooked in the telling of his scientific legacy. Much like Isaac Newton, the deep connection between Maxwell's faith and his scientific work has been downplayed in favor of focusing solely on his scientific rigor. While Maxwell's work continues to shape our understanding of the universe, the acknowledgment of his spiritual motivations has often been left out of the story.

Many of these men of God received divine inspiration, shaping the course of history with their innovations and ideas. However, their contributions were often stolen, overlooked, or separated from the faith that inspired them. The raiders of the Kingdom have long sought to take the fruit of divine wisdom without honoring the source from which it came. Today, we must recognize the importance of giving credit to the true source of wisdom and innovation—God Himself—and reclaim the Kingdom's treasures that have been unjustly taken. In doing so, we acknowledge the power of the Wonderful Counselor, who continues to inspire His people with visions and ideas that can change the world for the better.

Matthew 11:12 reveals a profound truth that echoes through the ages: from the moment John the Baptist began to proclaim the coming of the Kingdom, it has been under siege. The Kingdom of Heaven—God's divine storehouse of wisdom, creativity, and truth—has been attacked and raided by those who seek its treasures without acknowledging the Giver. These "violent men" have taken the revelations, the inspiration, and the power that belong to God's people and used them for their own capitalistic gain, presenting them to the world as if they were their own. By contrast, the truly altruistic who seek the Kingdom tend to give God the glory for all of their inspirations and insights.

An altruistic mind is a state of motivation where a person's goal is to improve the welfare of another person. Altruism is the opposite of egoism, which is the motivation to improve one's own welfare.

Some research suggests that altruism is deeply rooted in human nature. Studies have found that people's first impulse is to cooperate rather than compete. When people behave altruistically, their brains activate in regions that signal pleasure and reward.

Some examples of altruistic behavior include: Donating money to an organization, Starting a nonprofit, Picking up trash at a park Bringing refreshments to a school event, and, creating innovations for the betterment of mankind over profit.

In the intricate tapestry of human society, the conditions under which altruistic minds can flourish vary greatly across different systems. Capitalism, characterized by private ownership and the pursuit of profit, fosters innovation and economic growth. However, it often prioritizes individual success over collective welfare. This profit-driven model can create an environment where ethical considerations are secondary, leading to a culture that encourages competition at all costs. Also within this framework, resources and funding are typically channeled toward ventures that promise financial returns rather than community or environmental benefits. Socially conscious projects often struggle to secure financing or sustain themselves because their objectives—reducing inequality, improving education, or addressing climate change—do not always yield immediate or direct profit.

Some assume that "doing good" can easily be self-sustaining in the marketplace. But without profit as the primary motivator, socially beneficial projects often have limited access to capital, which makes long-term sustainability challenging. For socially conscious inventors and creators, this environment poses significant challenges. The relentless pursuit of financial gain can overshadow genuine desires to enact positive change, often resulting in frustration and disillusionment as they navigate a system that rewards exploitation rather than compassion.

Conversely, socialism emphasizes community welfare and collective ownership. In such societies, resources and wealth are distributed more equitably, promoting social safety nets and reducing the gap between the rich and poor. While this model supports the common good, the implementation can vary widely. In some cases, the bureaucracy may stifle individual creativity, limiting the potential for social entrepreneurs to flourish. Despite this, socialist societies generally create a more supportive framework for those with a heart for the greater good. By emphasizing cooperative ownership and community engagement, these nations foster an atmosphere where altruistic endeavors are not only encouraged but also rewarded.

Communism, on the other hand, seeks to eliminate private property entirely, with the state controlling all aspects of the economy. While the ideology aims for equality and community welfare, it often leads to severe restrictions on individual freedoms and innovation. The lack of incentives for personal achievement can stifle creativity, making it difficult for socially responsible initiatives to thrive. Inventors and visionaries may find themselves constrained by bureaucratic limitations, hindering their ability to enact meaningful change. Thus, while the intention is to create a fair society, the reality can often be a stifling environment for altruism.

In a capitalist society, the potential for exploitation of innovations remains high. Individuals and corporations driven by profit may not hesitate to "borrow" ideas and solutions from those whose hearts are yielded to God and dedicated to the common good. The dynamic of capitalism often creates a landscape where the most successful are those who can navigate the system and capitalize on the creativity of others.

Capitalism tends to measure success by growth, market share, or profit margins, not by community impact, environmental benefit, or social justice achievements. This profit-focused measurement can undervalue or dismiss inventions and projects that prioritize human welfare over financial gain. Many people assume that financial success and social good naturally align, thinking that successful businesses can always integrate social or environmental benefits. But in practice, companies often face shareholder pressure to maximize profit at the expense of community and ecological responsibilities.

This can lead to a cycle where altruistic innovations are co-opted for profit, leaving the original creators feeling sidelined and unsupported in their missions. As the kingdom of Heaven comes under siege from the relentless pursuits of capitalism, the visionaries who strive to enact positive change while giving honor to God, often struggle to protect their contributions.

So then, there is a cosmic struggle at play on the very globe we reside. The world we live in is not neutral ground. Since the days of John the Baptist, there has been an ongoing battle—a violent attempt to seize the Kingdom of Heaven's riches. The world's capitalists, wise men, those who refuse to bow before the Creator, have attempted to steal divine insight, passing it off as their own genius. They have raided the altruistic treasures of the Kingdom—wisdom, creativity, beauty—and used them for personal profit, writing books, producing movies, composing music, creating plays, and telling stories that leave out the very source of their inspiration.

But those of us who have accepted Jesus Christ as our Savior, who have received the Holy Spirit—the Wonderful Counselor—are now called to take back what has been stolen. The Kingdom of Heaven is ours to inherit. The divine insights and creative genius that have been raided by those who deny God must be reclaimed by His people. The wisdom and truth that flow from the Throne of Heaven were never meant to be perverted or misused for only capitalistic worldly gain. They were intended to glorify the Creator, to lead His people, and to draw the world closer to Him.

Capitalism often views altruism or social good as "nice to have" but not necessarily viable for achieving lasting success. Social en-trepreneurs or individuals driven by altruism may face skepticism about their financial sustainability or relevance, with investors view-ing them as high-risk. Many people assume nonprofits rely solely on charity rather than seeing them as strategic players in addressing so-cial problems. This stereotype can cause underfunding, less public support, and even undervaluing of career opportunities within these organizations.

The American Dream, often defined as individual success through hard work, can clash with the ethos of social consciousness, which prioritizes communal over personal gains. Socially conscious individ-uals may face cultural pushback if they focus on collective welfare rather than individual achievement. It implies that anyone can suc-ceed through hard work, often ignoring systemic barriers that inhibit equitable access to resources. Those who prioritize humanity over profit may encounter the misconception that they're avoiding traditional measures of success, when, in fact, they're working to overcome structural inequities.

It is time to take back the Kingdom of Heaven. This is your call-to-action. As a believer, you are not just an observer in this world; you are an active participant in God's unfolding plan. The treasures of the Kingdom belong to you. The wisdom, creativity, and spiritual wealth that have been raided are your inheritance through Christ. As the Wonderful Counselor dwells within you, you have access to the mind of Christ, the source of all creativity, power, and truth.

Now is the time to reclaim what has been stolen. Now is the time to rise up and create with boldness, giving credit where credit is due—to the King of Kings. Whether you write, sing, compose, paint, teach, or lead, let it be known that the treasures of the Kingdom of Heaven flow from the Spirit of God. You have the authority, through Christ, to manifest the beauty, wisdom, and power of the Kingdom in every area of life.

Let us take back the Kingdom. Let us walk in the fullness of what has been given to us by our Father, knowing that every good and perfect gift comes from Him. And as we reclaim the treasures that have been raided, let us honor the source—our Savior, our Wonderful Counselor—so that the world may see and know the One who is the true Author of every good thing.

| 4 |

Mining The Subconscious Mind's Ultimate Birthright

Tap into the hidden treasures of your Subconscious Mind, guided by the Mind of Christ, and discover how to manifest tangible success beyond your wildest dreams.

The power of the Subconscious Mind is immeasurable, yet it remains unmined by most of humanity. It holds the key to unlocking the spiritual frequencies that allow us to connect with divine truth and bring forth the Matter manifestation of God's promises. But to truly access this power, we must align our thoughts with the Mind of Christ, which governs the ultimate creative process of the universe. Through this connection, we are no longer bound by the limitations of the conscious mind or the temporal world, but instead, we gain access to the infinite resources of heaven.

The Mind of Christ is the divine template through which all creation flows. By synchronizing our subconscious mind with this heavenly blueprint, we begin to operate on a higher frequency, one that transcends the carnal mind and taps into the spiritual forces that shape reality. This spiritual alignment allows us to receive downloads of wisdom, direction, and divine inspiration directly from heaven, bypassing the noise of doubt and fear that plagues the Conscious Mind.

This is the foundation of walking in the spirit in true faith—NOW Faith, a faith that operates in the present moment and ignites the process of creation through God's Authority, Dominion, And Might (ADAM). But to activate this level of spiritual connection, we must become Matter Miners.

In today's world, the concept of mining has taken on new dimensions. Just as gold and diamonds are excavated from the earth after tremendous effort, another form of mining has emerged—Bitcoin mining. Unlike traditional mining, Bitcoin mining is a digital process where computers solve complex algorithms to release virtual coins. The value of Bitcoin is directly tied to how much of it has been mined. The scarcer it becomes, the more valuable it is. Similarly, in the spiritual realm, we are called to be Matter Miners, diligently mining the thoughts and wisdom of God to bring forth the Matter we seek to manifest in our lives. This divine Matter is just as valuable, if not more so, than gold, diamonds, or Bitcoin, and the process by which we mine it is rooted in the dynamic laws of attraction and creation.

In the same way that a Bitcoin Miner must consistently work, solving equations to uncover the digital wealth hidden in cyberspace, a Matter Miner must dig deep into the Word of God, the ultimate source of wisdom. But here's the thing: the Matter we are mining is not limited by earthly resources or digital scarcity. It is limitless, abundant, and accessible to all who are willing to Mine for it with NOW Faith. The process of spiritual Mining involves uncovering divine ideas, solutions, and images from the Mind of Christ through meditation, prayer, praise, worship, warfare and faith-filled declarations.

Just as miners spend years in pursuit of diamonds, extracting them from the dark depths of the earth, the Matter Miner must venture into the deep recesses of the Mind of Christ—where the treasures of wisdom and revelation reside. Diamonds are formed under immense pressure and heat, and Bitcoin is Mined through endless computing power. In the same way, we must invest the time, energy, and focus to receive the divine images God has stored for us. These images are like gold and diamonds, hidden treasures waiting for us to Mine them out through persistence and dedication.

Many Christians today, however, miss the process. They expect God to instantly deliver their Matter—whether it's a financial break-through, healing, or success—without any effort on their part. They pray for Matter and expect it to materialize like magic. This mentality treats God like a magician, and prayers are viewed like fast-food orders—expecting answers by the time their spiritual microwave reaches zero. But God operates differently. He is not a magician grant-ing us shortcuts. He is the God of all-wisdom, and He desires us to Mine His dynamic laws, truths, insights, and divine downloads through meditation on His Word and engaging the Mind of Christ.

> *"It is the glory of God to conceal a matter,*
> *But the glory of kings is to search out a matter."*
> (Proverbs 25:2 KJV)

God doesn't hide these treasures to keep them from us; He hides them so we can discover them and grow in our understanding and re-lationship with Him. He places Dynamic Secrets within the folds of His Word and creation, secrets that are only uncovered when we put in the work to Mine them out. God wants us to understand that there is a process to receiving our desires. Seed time and harvest time are foundational principles. If you pray for a mighty oak, you must under-stand that it may take decades to grow. The Matter Miner who seeks the fruits of wisdom, purpose, and revelation must be patient, know-ing that the process of Matter Mining requires time, persistence, and trust in God's timing.

In the same way that Bitcoin is mined over time—where each coin becomes more valuable as the pool of available coins diminishes—so too does the Matter we seek become more precious as we Mine it through NOW Faith. Every word we speak in NOW Faith serves as the magnetic force that attracts the protons, electrons, and neutrons, which coalesce to form atoms. These atoms then bind together to create molecules, and these molecules further attract one another, forming the Matter of our desires immediately in the spiritual unseen realm as we release the words. This entire process is governed by seed time and harvest time and will manifest in the physical to the diligent gardener. The Matter Miner knows that the key is persistence, just as a Bitcoin Miner continues Mining for what is valuable. The result is worth the process.

Just like the farmer planting his seed in the morning and staying busy all afternoon, we too must continuously speak the Word of God and meditate on His promises, allowing NOW Faith to do its work. Ecclesiastes reminds us, *"Plant your seed in the morning and keep busy all afternoon, for you do not know if profit will come from one activity, or another—or maybe both"* (Ecclesiastes 11:6). The Matter Miner understands that every act of NOW faith, every moment of prayer, and every word of meditation contributes to the ultimate manifestation of Matter.

But much like Bitcoin mining requires the solving of complex equations, the mining of Matter requires focus and intentionality. There will be distractions, doubts, and obstacles along the way. The enemy will attempt to plant weeds in your field—doubts, fears, and unbelief—to hinder your harvest. Jesus spoke of this in the parable of the wheat and the tares. While you are diligently planting seeds of NOW Faith, the enemy is waiting for you to fall asleep in your meditation, planting weed seeds that will choke out your harvest if you aren't careful. *"The Kingdom of Heaven is like a man who sowed good seed in his field. But while everyone was sleeping, his enemy came and sowed weeds among the wheat and went away"* (Matthew 13:24-28 NIV).

This is why it's critical for the Matter Miner to stay alert, consistent, and persistent. Meditation on the Word of God day and night is the key to ensuring that no weed seeds take root in your subconscious. The Subconscious Mind, when properly aligned with the Mind of Christ, becomes a receiver for divine thoughts, images, and wisdom. But just as a Bitcoin Miner must maintain their rig to solve each algorithm, the Matter Miner must continually refine their NOW Faith through meditation, prayer, and the Word of God.

The process of Matter Mining leads us to manifest our deepest desires—those that are aligned with God's will—by tuning our Subconscious Mind to the Mind of Christ. When we meditate, we receive the images and visions that reveal the divine Matter waiting to be Mined. Through our words of NOW Faith, we attract the Matter that manifests in our reality. Just like the slow process of mining Bitcoin, our desires manifest in alignment with seed time and harvest time.

The journey of a Matter Miner is one of faith, patience, and perseverance. It is not for the faint of heart, nor for those seeking instant gratification. But for those willing to put in the effort, to dig deep into the Word, to persist in NOW Faith, the reward is immeasurable. The Mind of Christ is the center of all creativity, and when we Mine His thoughts, we access the very blueprint of creation. The Matter Miner understands that this process is the essence of aligning with God's will, and through it, we gain the wisdom, understanding, and manifestation of the Matter we seek.

Now that we understand the mission of the Matter Miner, we must turn our attention to the language or frequencies of the two planes of thought.

Every human being operates within two distinct realms of thought—realms as separate as day and night, yet inextricably linked. These realms, the Conscious Mind and the Subconscious Mind, are like two different radio frequencies, each operating on its own bandwidth, undetectable to the other. To fully understand how these realms work in tandem, shaping our lives, imagine them as an AM and FM radio waves—each transmitting its own signals and broadcasting on a completely different frequency. Tuning into one realm or the other determines what you perceive, how you think, and ultimately, how you manifest the world around you.

The Conscious Mind, seated in the brain within the human skull, can be likened to an AM radio signal. It operates on the lower, more limited frequency of sensory input—focusing on what it can perceive through the Sarx five senses: sight, sound, touch, taste, and smell. The Conscious Mind deals with reason, logic, imagination, and short-term memory. It is wired to seek immediate gratification, to avoid pain and pursue pleasure, based entirely on the input it receives from the external world.

Like an AM radio, the Conscious Mind can only process one broadcast at a time, and it is often subject to interference—static and noise that come in the form of worry, doubt, fear, and external distractions. When tuned to this frequency, your thinking is reactive, grounded in the physical, and often limited by circumstance and logic. The Conscious Mind is where most people operate, making decisions based on what they see, hear, or experience at a surface level, unable to perceive the deeper layers of reality. It's driven by what is external, trying to reason out the physical world with limited tools.

AM signals travel farther in the open but are easily disrupted by interference, much like how the Conscious Mind is easily swayed by external stimuli—social pressures, negative influences, social media, TV streaming, and fleeting emotions. The Conscious Mind is where fear, doubt, and the clutter of everyday life reside, pulling you into a cycle of reactive thought patterns that limit your potential. When your focus is trapped within this realm, you become disconnected from the higher wisdom that lies beneath.

In contrast, the Subconscious Mind operates on a higher, more refined frequency, much like FM radio transmission. While AM signals are constrained by distance and prone to static, FM signals are clear, rich, and capable of carrying complex information over shorter, more powerful wavelengths. The Subconscious Mind, seated in the brain of the heart, is where both the core of your being and the Kingdom of God within you resides. It's the realm of infinite potential, where your true desires, beliefs, and convictions are held, and where spiritual revelation occurs.

"Around the early 1990's, researchers found that the heart had nerve cells or neurons that were akin to the ones that made up the brain. In other words, the heart had its very own nervous system that could function independently of the brain! Affectionately called "the little brain" of the heart, it became a point of fascination in the field—why does the heart need its own nervous system anyway? How does it help the heart function? It also became a potential target for the vagus nerve. Could a connection between the brain and the "little brain" be the key to restoring heart health?

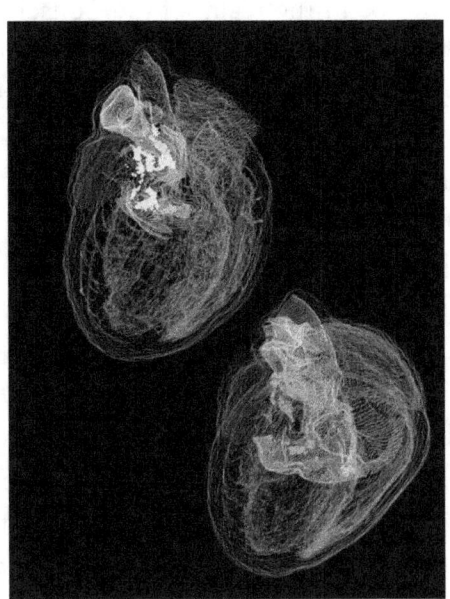

Male vs. Female: A comparison of the "little brain" in the male heart (yellow dots) and female heart (pink dots). The distribution of the neurons is different, and there are fewer neurons in the female heart.

Images captured by Shaina Robbins, MS

Drs. Schwaber and Vadigepalli have been at the forefront of trying to answer these questions for the last 25 years, giving critical insight into the heart's nervous system. In the last five years, serendipity brought them together with like-minded experts and advanced technology that allowed a major breakthrough: the first ever 3D map of the heart's "little brain."

Operating beyond the noise of external stimuli, the Subconscious Mind, within this "little brain" of the heart, is always connected to the divine—the frequency of the Kingdom of God and the Mind of Christ. It processes information not through sensory input but through prayer, discernment, intuition, praise, worship, faith, spiritual revelation, and a sense of just knowing. This realm is not reactive like the Conscious Mind; it is creative. It is the seat of your long-term memory, your beliefs, your habits, and most importantly, your spiritual frequency. It is where Spirit to spirit transference happens. *"God is spirit [the Source of life, yet invisible to mankind], and those who worship Him must worship in spirit and truth."* (John 4:24 AMP)

Therefore, one cannot say that they may violate the Law of Worship by feelings and emotions. The Law is quite clear, for true and effective worship to God, you cannot be in the realm of the Conscious Mind, the realm of your Sarx flesh, it must be to and from the quite place within your spirit, the seat of your Sub Conscious Mind. First, we must acknowledge that God is Spirit, and, hence, He is not tied to one location, not confined by time nor space for our worship. Second, we must worship according to the truth of Jesus' person and work, for He is the truth and, thus, the only way whereby we may truly worship God. *"Jesus told him, "I am the way, the truth, and the life. No one can come to the Father except through me."* (John 14:6 KJV)

The Subconscious Mind is also not confined by time, space, or circumstance. Just as FM radio produces clearer, more powerful sound waves, the Subconscious Mind transmits and receives signals to and from the Kingdom without distortion. This is where the "still small voice" of the Wonderful Counselor can be heard, unobstructed by the interference of the world. It's where manifestations of your desires take shape, and where NOW faith can transform accepted thoughts and images into reality.

When you tune into this frequency, you're no longer confined to the logic and limitations of the Conscious Mind. You have and infinite freedom to access higher levels of understanding, where NOW faith and belief becomes Matter, and where the Dynamic Laws of Attraction, Creation, and Manifestation are engaged. You become in sync with divine wisdom, pulling down heavenly ideas, images, and insights into your everyday life.

Though these two realms operate on different frequencies, they are intertwined in shaping the reality you experience. The Conscious Mind can influence the Subconscious Mind by planting seeds—thoughts and beliefs that, if nurtured, will manifest in the physical world. The thoughts you focus on or entertain in the Conscious Mind are transmitted to the Subconscious Mind, where they take root, grow, and eventually produce a harvest—good or bad. This is why what you dwell on consciously can profoundly impact your destiny.

It should be no surprise that the unseen enemy of your soul uses the very same immutable laws that govern the universe to plant his weed seeds in your garden of life via the AM conscious transmission. Why, because he and his cohorts KNOW they work. They know the Law of Seed Time and Harvest Time will always work as long as this earth remains, and is the sensory access to his Conscious Mind, where warped religious beliefs wrapped in emotionalism will ultimately be accepted into his Subconscious Mind.

And here is the biggest dilemma for the believers, the AM Transmission weed planted strongholds from the enemy while you slept, were added immediately after God's FM Transmission word was received, if you uttered your acceptance of them aloud. The spirit of religion being preached, the law and grace mixed, is the greatest cause of the new and old covenants canceling each other out so that you try to live your faith walk under both. *"And no man putteth new wine into old bottles; else the new wine will burst the bottles, and be spilled, and the bottles shall perish. But new wine must be put into new bottles; and both are preserved. No man also having drunk old wine straightway desireth new: for he saith, The old is better."* (Luke 5:37-39 KJV)

In Jesus's day, people used animal skins-like goatskin-for storing liquids. Fermented drinks like wine expanded, and since an old wineskin would already be stretched to its limit, the new wine would tear the seams. This is why new wine needed to be preserved in new wineskins. However, an old bottle will not stretch, yield, and respond to the gas pressure developed by the fermenting wine. Because the old bottle will not stretch, it will just explode. Then, both the bottle and wine are lost. Therefore, new wine also needs to be put into new bottles.

This parable illustrates that new wine should be put into new bottles, not old ones, because the old bottles will not stretch or respond to the pressure from the fermenting wine and will burst. The parable also shows that both the wine and the bottle will be lost if the new wine is put into an old bottle.

The parable is often interpreted to mean that new ideas or things should be put into new structures that are flexible enough to accommodate them. If the structure is not flexible enough, it will not be able to hold the new thing and will break, causing the new thing to run out. This is where when God instructs that He is doing "a new thing" will often collide with the thinking "the old way is better". New and old wine cannot mix no more that religious teachings that try to bind new people under grace to an old go-getter practice of the law. The law of Moses is for the learning for the new receivers of The Law of Love, often referred to as grace, restored by Jesus' sacrifice, not to be bound those old commands as an active way of trying to live them out.

"And thou shalt love the Lord thy God with all thy heart, and with all thy soul, and with all thy mind, and with all thy strength: this is the first commandment. And the second is like, namely this, Thou shalt love thy neighbour as thyself. There is none other commandment greater than these." (Mark 12:30-31 KJV)

"Owe no man any thing, but to love one another: for he that loveth another hath fulfilled the law. For this, Thou shalt not commit adultery, Thou shalt not kill, Thou shalt not steal, Thou shalt not bear false witness, Thou shalt not covet; and if there be any other commandment, it is briefly comprehended in this saying, namely, Thou shalt love thy neighbour as thyself. Love worketh no ill to his neighbour: therefore love is the fulfilling of the law." (Romans 13:8-10 KJV)

Jesus uses another metaphor, in Mark 2:22, that of new wine and old skins, to illustrate why He does not lead His disciples to follow the religion under the Law of the Pharisees, specifically in fasting. Old wineskins, like the Pharisees' rules, are brittle and inflexible. It was Jesus' intention that His followers use the Book of the Law as informational to meditate on day and night for their learning, but that they would live their lives under His finished work over the Law of Love under grace. Not preach to live under both requirements, just one.

Imagine trying to listen to both the FM and AM radio playing at the same time. What a ball of confusion that would be. But that is exactly what vacillating between the AM fear-filled words of the Sarx and the FM faith-filled words of the Spirit does to most people. It is why, in the parable of the good ground Sower, some received 30-fold, some 60 and some 100-fold what they sowed. Fear will cause you to say things Faith will not, and saying is sowing according to the word. *"Do not be deceived, God is not mocked; for whatever a man sows, that he will also reap. For he who sows to his flesh will of the flesh reap corruption, but he who sows to the Spirit will of the Spirit reap everlasting life."* (Galatians 6:7-8 NKJV)

The Law is only for your learning reference and not to govern your life in Christ by. Members of the faith family who has received Christ as Messiah, are no longer bound by the law, but free from it. Not free to violate the law, but free from its, impossible-to-fulfill judgment, against all sin. These AM religious whispers from the unseen realm, (sometimes through or preachers under that influence) bring guilt and shame to the people because of these broken laws against sin that history has proven, no one can perfectly keep.

So, this is why it is important that you tune in to the higher frequency of the Subconscious Mind—the FM signal, if you will—requires more than just conscious thought. It requires stillness, meditation, faith, and intentionality. It requires aligning your spirit with the Spirit of God, transcending the distractions and noise of the world to receive divine guidance. *"For the Kingdom of God is within you."*

Most people remain stuck in the lower-frequency realm of the Conscious Mind, struggling against the static of fear, doubt, and external pressures. But those who learn to tune their minds to the higher frequency of the Subconscious—the realm of NOW faith, divine inspiration, and spiritual discernment—are the ones who access real power, the kind that transforms lives, manifests abundance, and fulfills destinies.

The heart, as the Bible says, is where the issues of life flow from. *"Guard your heart, for everything you do flows from it"* (Proverbs 4:23). The Subconscious Mind and the Kingdom of God, seated in the heart, is the gateway to accessing the divine frequency of the Wonderful Counselor. It is the place where God plants His will, vision, desires, dreams, images, and plans for you.

But the enemy knows this too. Just as there are raiders of the Kingdom, there are forces that aim to keep you tuned in to the lower-frequency AM realm of the Conscious Mind. These forces come in the spiritual form of doubt, fear, and external distractions, designed to steal the blessings that are meant for you. When you allow your Conscious Mind to take in and dwell on negative thoughts, you inadvertently shift the Subconscious Mind's frequency to align with those very doubts and fears, canceling out the faith-filled words and images that the Wonderful Counselor has already begun to manifest.

Victory, then, lies in your ability to keep your thoughts and mouth attuned to the higher frequency. The last one to leave the battlefield—the one who remains steadfast in NOW faith and conviction—wins the battle of manifestation. You must stay tuned to the frequency of the Spirit, refusing to allow the static of the Conscious

Mind to disrupt the transmission of divine revelation and manifestation.

In understanding these two realms of thought, you hold the key to shaping your reality. What will you tune in to? The AM world of doubt, fear, and limitation? Or the FM frequency of faith, abundance, vast wealth, and divine wisdom? The choice is yours, and the power lies in your ability to stay connected to the higher realm—the realm of the Subconscious Mind where the Mind of Christ operates in full authority. Choose wisely, and watch the power of divine attraction transform your life.

| 5 |

Manifesting God's Promises:
The Law of Attraction

*U*ncover the powerful connection between your thoughts and God's *promises through the Dynamic Law of Attraction and watch His plans unfold.*

In the vast tapestry of the universe, there exists a principle as old as creation itself—the Law of Attraction. This law asserts that like attracts like; our thoughts, feelings, and beliefs draw corresponding experiences into our lives. While many perceive it as a mere tool for personal gain, its roots and implications delve much deeper, intertwining with our spiritual journey and alignment with God's will.

Everything in the universe is the result of thought. Every invention was first conceived on the plane of thought, first as an image in the mind of the inventor and then materialized as a result of that thought. The creative heart-brain of the Subconscious Mind acts on all volitional thoughts that is placed there. This heart-mind begins to manifest all thoughts picked up from the Conscious Mind into reality to the person thinking it.

Every atom, every particle, vibrates with a purpose, responding to the frequencies set forth by the Everlasting Father. As believers, we are invited to understand and engage with this dynamic interplay, tapping into the Law of Attraction to manifest God's promises in our lives.

The Law of Attraction, when understood in its divine context, reveals that our thoughts and beliefs shape our reality. The formed atom sets up a vibration, seeking out others with similar vibrations. Similarly, our thoughts emit frequencies that attract corresponding thinking and experiences into our lives. When our thought lives are aligned with the Mind of Christ, we tap into the dynamic power that governs the universe.

However, many of us struggle to manifest God's promises due to internal barriers, the strongholds. These barriers are negative thought patterns and beliefs rooted in fear, doubt, superstition, and past traumas. They act as obstacles that prevent us from fully engaging with the Law of Attraction. For instance, if someone harbors a subconscious belief in scarcity, they may continually experience lack, despite consciously desiring abundance.

To overcome these strongholds, we must diligently acknowledge their presence. Recognizing negative patterns in our lives is the initial step toward dismantling them. Next, we must renew our minds by immersing ourselves in God's Word, replacing false beliefs with His truths. As Romans 12:2 (NIV) advises, *"Do not conform to the pattern of this world, but be transformed by the renewing of your mind."* Affirming God's promises through prayer and meditation reinforces this transformation, allowing us to align our Subconscious Mind with divine intentions.

The Law of Attraction isn't just a modern-day concept; its roots run deep in the teachings of the Bible. Scripture repeatedly affirms that our thoughts hold the power to shape our reality. In Proverbs 23:7, we find this undeniable truth: *"For as he thinks in his heart, so is he."* What you meditate on, what you believe deep within yourself, becomes the fabric of your life. Your thoughts don't just hover in your mind—they manifest, creating the circumstances and experiences you encounter. The spiritual Law of Sowing and Reaping starts in the mind. When we allow the right seeds of thought to take root, they will inevitably grow into the harvest of our reality, shaping everything around us into our desires.

Jesus Himself reinforced these laws. In Matthew 7:7, He tells us, *"Ask, and it will be given to you; seek, and you will find; knock, and it will be opened to you."* Here lies the powerful truth of intention. What you ask for, when pursued with unyielding NOW faith, will come to pass. This is not idle wishing—this is the law of focused pursuit aligned with divine timing. But the key that unlocks all of this is belief. In Mark 11:24, Jesus lays it out clearly: *"Whatever you ask in prayer, believe that you have received it, and it will be yours."* It is belief that pulls what is in the unseen into the seen, that calls what is not yet into existence. These scriptures are not just stories—they are laws, guiding us to understand that faith-filled thoughts backed by the Mind of Christ are the force that brings our desires into reality.

The first step to activating the Law of Attraction is to meditate on God's promises. This is more than just a quiet moment of reflection and chanting; it's about immersing yourself daily in the scriptures that affirm God's love, His favor, and His plans for your life and rolling them over and over in your mind. When you fill your mind with God's Word, you plant seeds of abundance, joy, and victory in the fertile ground of the thoughts of your heart brain. Verses like Jeremiah 29:11 remind us that His plans are to prosper us and give us hope. Take these promises and let them saturate your mind until they become the foundation of your belief system. As you meditate, you align your mind with the Mind of Christ, allowing the Subconscious Mind to accept and nurture these truths, and from that alignment, the dynamic Law of Life in Christ Jesus begin to work in your favor.

Next, you must learn to visualize with clarity. This is where the power of thought manifests into reality. Envision yourself living in the fulfillment of God's promises—walking in health, success, and spiritual abundance. See yourself in the midst of blessings, not merely hoping but knowing that what you see in your mind's eye is already yours. Visualization isn't daydreaming; it's a focused, faith-filled practice that draws the unseen into the seen. When you visualize with conviction, you're not just thinking of possibilities—you're bringing them into reality. This clarity of vision is the blueprint that the Mind of Christ works with to manifest God's promises in your life.

But visualization alone isn't enough. You must also maintain a positive and targeted confession. The words you speak reflect the state of your faith. Homologeō means to say the same thing. The logeō part is "say" or "speak." Together, the word has the literal meaning of "to say the same thing." In the New Testament, homologeō is often translated as "confess" or "confession." Or better put, to confess about yourself the promises God has confessed over you.

When we speak, we should align our words with the promises God has already spoken over us, allowing our confession to mirror His truth. Just as God's Word carries creative power and authority, our words, when aligned with His, carry the same force to manifest His promises in our lives. It's not merely about speaking positively but about declaring what God has already declared, knowing that His Word is never spoken in vain. The power behind this truth is revealed in the authority and certainty of God's word—it never returns empty or void but accomplishes everything He intends.

"So shall my word be that goeth forth out of my mouth: it shall not return unto me void, but it shall accomplish that which I please, and it shall prosper in the thing whereto I sent it." (Isaiah 55:11 KJV)

Speak life, speak victory, and speak God's incorruptible word seeds into every situation. When doubt or negativity try to creep in as "heard" thoughts, ideas and suggestions, reject them with the power of the written words of God, just as Jesus did. Jesus, having come to earth in the flesh, was also subject to the same temptations and suggestions of the devil by hearing it in His own head, just as every other human.

I know, movies like to portray the devil as some big bad figure in a red suit with a pitchfork. But if that's how he showed up, wouldn't we easily recognize him and dismiss his voice as something foreign to our normal way of thinking? Instead, he tempts us in subtle ways, using the same vain questionings he posed to Eve in the garden and to Jesus after His baptism by John. Just like then, he comes right after the word has been spoken over our lives—his goal is always to kill, steal, and destroy. Pay attention to the scriptures in Luke where the conversational exchange between speaking and hearing is very real, occurring on the plane of thought. This is the space where released thinking seeks to attract like thinking, taking root and creating matter. We must stay alert to these "weed seeds" the enemy tries to plant and grow weeds or steal Matter through his questions and suggestions.

"And Jesus being full of the Holy Ghost returned from Jordan, and was led by the Spirit into the wilderness, Being forty days tempted of the devil. And in those days he did eat nothing: and when they were ended, he afterward hungered. **And the devil** _said_ **unto him,** _If thou be the Son of God,_ *command this stone that it be made bread.* **And Jesus** _answered_ **him,** _saying,_ (Not Thinking, but SAYING – homologeō) **It is written,** *That man shall not live by bread alone, but by every word of God. And the devil, taking him up into an high mountain, shewed unto him all the kingdoms of the world in a moment of time.* **And the devil** _said_ **unto him,** *All this power will I give thee, and the glory of them: for that is delivered unto me; and to whomsoever I will I give it.* _If thou therefore wilt worship me,_ *all shall be*

*thine. **And Jesus <u>answered</u> and <u>said</u> unto him**, Get thee behind me, Satan: **for it is written**, Thou shalt worship the Lord thy God, and him only shalt thou serve. And he brought him to Jerusalem, and set him on a pinnacle of the temple, and **<u>said</u>** unto him, <u>If thou be the Son of God</u>, cast thyself down from hence: **<u>For it is written</u>*** (devil speaking bible now, but out of context *he knows the power of Gods Words too), *He shall give his angels charge over thee, to keep thee: And in their hands they shall bear thee up, lest at any time thou dash thy foot against a stone. **And Jesus <u>answering</u> <u>said</u> unto him**, It is said, Thou shalt not tempt the Lord thy God. And when the devil had ended all the temptation, he departed from him for a season. And Jesus returned in the power of the Spirit into Galilee: and there went out a fame of him through all the region round about."* (Luke 4:1-14 KJV)

As Proverbs 18:21 says, *"Death and life are in the power of the tongue."* When you confess an answer to the weed seed conversations of thought, you attract those lies and create death from your own tongue. Your words must reflect the homologeō NOW faith words of life you hold in your heart. And as you confess positivity in the promises, the action in NOW faith becomes automatic. Faith without works is dead, but NOW faith in motion, aligned with the Mind of Christ, attracts the blessings you seek.

Surround yourself with like-minded believers, those who will lift you up and not tear you down. Your environment matters, and the company you keep will either fuel your NOW faith or reinforce your Strongholds. Choose wisely, and you will see how God uses these relationships to elevate your journey of NOW faith. Your relationships are not just surface-level connections; they are spiritual influences that shape the depth of your belief system.

Romans 12:2 urges us: *"Do not conform to the pattern of this world but be transformed by the renewing of your mind."* This renewal is not just a conscious effort but a deep subconscious transformation that aligns our entire being with God's purposes. Negative strongholds hinder us from experiencing God's fullness. These strongholds can sabotage our efforts to manifest our desires, even when we consciously strive for positive outcomes.

As a human being, you will make mistakes in arriving at truth. Do not allow remorse to become a stronghold. Be joyful that error has disclosed truth. Confess your sins, and God, who is faithful, will forgive you and cleanse you of all unrighteousness. That's the end of the transaction. It's over. You only have the dynamic effect to deal with, the cause it set in motion, but the transgression is squashed. So, you must not continue in remorse one-minute past confession.

The tragic picture of a man dragging through life, chastising himself for every mistake, making discouragement and shame his companion, and is a major source and cause of many strongholds of the Subconscious Mind. Let us not be afraid of making a mistake or of suffering the consequence if the mistake is made. Just be sure to get the lesson from the mistake, that way you only have to suffer the consequence of each mistake only once and no more.

The process of manifesting God's promises involves several practical steps. Meditating on Scripture allows God's truths to permeate our minds, establishing a solid foundation. Speaking life by declaring God's promises reinforces our faith and sends out corresponding like vibrations. Visualizing our desires in alignment with the received image and God's will helps to focus our intentions. Cultivating gratitude shifts our perspective from lack to abundance, further attracting blessings into our lives. Lastly, maintaining unwavering NOW faith, even in the face of challenges, keeps us aligned with God's Dynamic Laws.

Embracing the Dynamic Law of Attraction requires us to exercise the authority given to us through Christ. By installing the Positive Throne of Authority, Dominion, and Might (ADAM) in our Subconscious Minds, we replace negative strongholds with divine empowerment. This Throne is established when we accept and believe in God's covenant promises, allowing us to operate from a place of spiritual Authority, Dominion, and Might.

As we align our thoughts with God's will in NOW faith, we begin to see His promises manifest in our lives. Health, provision, peace, and purpose become realities rather than distant hopes. We experience the abundant life that Jesus spoke of in John 10:10 (NIV): "*I have come that they may have life, and have it to the full.*"

Let us, therefore, embrace this profound truth and step into the fullness of what God has prepared for us. As Jesus assured us, greater works are within our reach when we believe and align ourselves with Him.

At the genesis of time, God spoke the universe into existence. His words were not random utterances but powerful vibrations that materialized into reality. As beings created in His image and after His likeness (Genesis 1:27), we too possess the innate ability to shape our reality through our thoughts and words. "*For as he thinks in his heart, so is he.*" This isn't just poetic expression; it's a divine revelation about the creative powerful law embedded within us.

When we align our thoughts and beliefs with God's truth, we don't just transform our own lives; we become conduits of His love and bring power to the world. Our lives become testimonies of His grace, drawing others towards the light. The Law of Attraction, rooted in divine law, enables us to fulfill our destinies and impact those around us positively.

The very fabric of the universe reflects this divine Dynamic Law. Atoms, the fundamental building blocks of Matter, set up vibrations and seek out other atoms with corresponding frequencies. In this coalescence of units vibrating on the same frequency, Matter as we know it in our physical world is formed. Thus, Matter is born from intelligence; more importantly, intelligence resides within Matter—in fact, <u>intelligence is Matter</u>. Since intelligence implies consciousness, it follows that we are surrounded by a living universe, imbued with consciousness in all things.

Jesus hinted at this profound reality when the Pharisees attempted to silence His followers:

"Then some of the Pharisees in the crowd spoke to Jesus. 'Teacher,' they said, 'command your disciples to be quiet!' Jesus answered, 'I tell you that if they keep quiet, the stones themselves will start shouting.'"
(Luke 19:39-40 GNT)

Here, Jesus acknowledges that even the stones possess a form of consciousness capable of responding to God's glory.

Another illustration of this principle is found in the story of Elisha and the floating ax head:

"As one of them was cutting down a tree, suddenly his iron ax head fell in the water. 'What shall I do, sir?' he exclaimed to Elisha. 'It was a borrowed ax!' 'Where did it fall?' Elisha asked. The man showed him the place, and Elisha cut off a stick, threw it in the water, and made the ax head float. 'Take it out,' he ordered, and the man reached down and picked it up."
(2 Kings 6:5-7 GNT)

In this miraculous event, thought calls form into existence. The very intelligence within the atoms of the ax head responds to Elisha's actions, demonstrating the interconnectedness of thought, Matter, and divine power.

Even Thomas Edison was intrigued by the mysterious behavior of atoms. He pondered what he termed "the obvious choice of the atom" in its infinite acceptances and rejections within chemical combinations. When two chemicals are mixed, certain atoms combine while others do not. Edison questioned why specific atoms would choose to bond with certain others. The only conceivable answer was that atoms possess a form of consciousness — the ability to make choices about their interactions.

In the context of Elisha's miracle, the atoms forming the iron ax head "chose" to be attracted to the atoms of the cut stick that Elisha threw into the water. Through the Mind of Christ, Elisha received divine guidance on how to activate this atomic attraction. The atom, as a center of force, is conscious and responsive to spiritual authority.

Working in accordance with divine law—through the Mind of Christ—the atom seeks out other atoms vibrating at a corresponding rate and coalesces into molecules, forming what we designate as inanimate Matter: water, earth, air, trees, and minerals. Thus, the ax head floated toward the stick, defying natural expectations and affirming the power of spiritual laws over physical ones.

These examples illustrate that the Law of Attraction is not merely a metaphysical concept, but divine Dynamic Laws woven into the very fabric of creation. When we align our thoughts and intentions with God's will, we tap into these Dynamic Laws, enabling us to manifest His promises in our lives. Our thoughts, like the vibrations of atoms, attract corresponding realities. By cultivating a consciousness rooted in faith and aligned with the Mind of Christ, we participate in the ongoing creation and transformation of the world around us.

Every thought we harbor emits a spiritual frequency, resonating with similar energies in the universe. Positive, God inspired faith-filled thoughts and words align us with God's abundance, drawing blessings and opportunities. Conversely, negative thoughts and released words rooted in fear, doubt, or resentment will eventually attract undesirable experiences. It's imperative to recognize that our minds are not just processing units but broadcasting stations, sending out signals that shape our destiny.

Even the greatest recorded, unrepeated, miracle in the bible – Jesus walking on water can be categorized into the immutable Dynamic Law of Attraction and coalescence of the molecules of water, air, and the body. The proof – Peter also walked on the water, at least until he violated the Dynamic Law of (perfect) Love that casts out all fear. Once his thinking strayed, he considered the waves and the water, and no longer attracted the sustaining atoms and molecules in their place; he brought in the Stronghold of fear and doubt that any fisherman would have. And as quickly as one Dynamic Law worked, the next one with more conviction handed him exactly as he thought, and he began to sink.

Jesus did not want us to see these demonstrations of operating in perfect authority as something "only He" could do. *"Verily, verily, I say unto you, He that believeth on me, the works that I do shall he do also; and greater works than these shall he do; because I go unto my Father. And whatsoever ye shall ask in my name, that will I do, that the Father may be glorified in the Son. If ye shall ask any thing in my name, I will do it."* (John 14:12-14 KJV)

It's essential to approach the Law of Attraction with humility and reverence for God. It's not a magical formula or a means to bypass God's sovereignty. Our ultimate goal should be to glorify Him, not to idolize our desires. Remember the words of Jesus: *"But seek first the kingdom of God and His righteousness, and all these things shall be added to you"* (Matthew 6:33).

Each human being who lives is surrounded by a subtle but powerful thought atmosphere. We are accustomed to believing that thoughts are invisible, yet we mark the existence of thousands of them with our very eyes each day. The thoughts of each man stand written on his face, on his brow, in the expressions of his eyes, in the set of his lips, the carriage of his head, his posture, his bearing, his demeanor, in the tone of his conversation, his character, his successes, his failures, his very life. Let a man walk into a room where you are, and you immediately are conscious of the thought atmosphere that surrounds him.

Your very first reaction is that you either like him or you don't. It isn't the man that prompts you to this instinctive decision – it's the kind of thoughts he thinks! His mental atmosphere reaches out and contacts yours immediately. If it is similar, you are attracted to him. If it is opposed, you dislike him. Only a modification of thinking on the part of one or both of you can change this, for like gravitates to like in the universe and throughout all nature.

Each of us seeks for good to enter his life. Even when we become negative thinkers and hopeless and defeated, it is still good we seek – we think negatively while hoping for the positive. Patterns of cynical and negative thinking and speech seem our only means of coping with a world which appears bent on denying all our goals and aims and desires. These are our Strongholds, the yokes we bear that we do not cast upon the waiting Christ.

God denies us nothing. Nature denies us nothing. We always get exactly what we have asked for. There is no evil, lack, limitations, failure, or despair which we do not create for ourselves in our own minds. *"When tempted, no one should say, 'God is tempting me.' For God cannot be tempted by evil, nor does he tempt anyone; but each person is tempted when they are dragged away by their own evil desire and enticed.*

Then, after desire has conceived, it gives birth to sin; and sin, when it is full-grown, gives birth to death." (James 1:13-15 NIV)

And it is just as simple, in fact downright simpler, to create and accept abundance and success and health in our Subconscious Mind and thus experience them in the physical world. The great lesson we all must learn is to seek God's righteousness [right standing] that will renew our Conscious Minds to the infinite power and think positively for good. Seeking good and yet thinking evil, we destroy our lives on the sharp edge of the Dynamic Law of Attraction and manifestation.

The Law of Attraction is a divine mechanism, intricately woven into the fabric of creation. By understanding and applying it within the framework of our relationship with God, we unlock the doors to abundant living. Let us commit to purifying our thoughts, renewing our minds, and aligning our hearts with His. In doing so, we not only attract His blessings but also become blessings to others, fulfilling the higher calling placed upon our lives. We are blessed to be a blessing.

Our thoughts are more than fleeting ideas; they are powerful transmitters, sending signals into the spiritual realm. When our thinking aligns with God's Word, it sets in motion a divine frequency that attracts His blessings and draws us closer to His will. It's not enough to simply think passively—our thoughts must be intentional, filled with the life-giving power of God's promises. Proverbs 18:21 reminds us that *"death and life are in the power of the tongue,"* meaning that what we speak has both the power to create or destroy. This is why we must engage in positive confession, speaking words that breathe life, hope, and faith into every situation. Every word we release should reflect the homologeō promises God has already made over us, because in that confession, we activate the very blessings we're seeking.

But this process goes deeper than words. It requires the visualization of those promises as a current reality. This isn't idle daydreaming—this is NOW faith in action. See yourself walking in the victory God has promised, fully embracing the image of the person God has called you to be. Along with this, meditation on Scripture is essential. When we reflect deeply on the Word, allowing it to saturate our Subconscious Mind, we plant seeds that will grow into the fruitful manifestation of God's purpose for our lives. Every verse you meditate on becomes a foundation stone for the life you're building in Christ, anchoring your thoughts, your words, and your actions in divine truth.

NOW faith is the activating force that brings our desires into reality. Hebrews 11:1 defines faith as *"the substance of things hoped for, the evidence of things not seen."* Without faith, it's impossible to please God or to fully activate the Law of Attraction in our lives.

Building NOW faith requires intentional action, not passive belief. The first step is to hear the Word, for *"faith comes by hearing, and hearing by the Word of God"* (Romans 10:17). You can't develop strong NOW faith if you're not immersing yourself in God's truth, allowing His Word to shape your thoughts and guide your actions. But hearing alone is not enough. You must act on your belief, because as James 2:26 says, *"faith without works is dead."* True faith demands that you align your actions with what you profess to believe—your daily life should reflect the conviction of your NOW faith. And finally, you must persist in prayer, maintaining open communication with God, constantly seeking His guidance, and nurturing the relationship that strengthens your NOW faith. Prayer is the lifeline that keeps your faith grounded and growing, ensuring that your actions remain in alignment with His will.

Harnessing the Law of Attraction begins with setting clear intentions that are aligned with God's will. You must define what you truly desire, and ensure that these desires honor Him. Be specific in your requests—God is not a God of vague promises but of precision and purpose. He knows the plans He has for you, but you must partner with Him by making your intentions known. It's through this clarity that the power of attraction begins to work. However, intention alone is not enough. You must maintain a gratitude attitude, thanking God not only for what you have but also for what is yet to come. Gratitude raises your spiritual vibration and opens the floodgates for more blessings. It transforms your heart, positioning you to receive the very things you seek by attracting God's goodness into your life.

Alongside gratitude, you must eliminate doubt from your heart and mind. Doubt is the enemy of NOW faith and can block the flow of God's promises. Guard your mind against skepticism and negativity, just like the man who said to Jesus, *"Lord, I believe; help my unbelief!"* (Mark 9:24). This isn't about denying your challenges; it's about choosing to believe that God's word is more powerful than your circumstances. Surround yourself with a faithful community—believers who encourage and uplift you—because the company you keep will either strengthen your NOW faith or feed your doubts. And finally, stay obedient to God's Word, for it is obedience that opens the doors of opportunity that NOW faith has unlocked. Obedience aligns you with God's timing and plan, ensuring that what you've attracted through NOW faith is realized in His perfect way.

The Law of Attraction was never meant to be a tool for selfish ambition but a divine rule to fulfill God's purpose for your life. It's crucial to ensure that your desires are in alignment with His will. Jesus said, *"Seek first the kingdom of God and His righteousness, and all these things shall be added to you"* (Matthew 6:33). This means your priority must always be the pursuit of His kingdom, not just your own desires. When you align your heart with God's, the Matter you seek will naturally follow, because they're no longer driven by self, but by His will for you. Psalm 37:4 reminds us, *"Delight yourself also in the Lord, and He shall give you the desires of your heart."* When you truly delight in Him, your desires become reflections of His divine purpose. This means it is God who plants the desires in your heart that you probably thought were your own. They come from God and are no longer just wants—they are part of His plan to manifest His goodness in your life.

When our hearts are aligned with God, our planted desires become a natural extension of His will. It is the Holy Spirit who guides us into all truth, as John 16:13 reminds us, revealing what we may not see and leading us toward the fulfillment of God's perfect plan. The Spirit doesn't just inform us; He transforms our prayers, aligning them with the Father's will and empowering us to overcome the weaknesses that hinder our NOW faith. To truly walk in this alignment, we must listen to His guidance—spending quiet, intentional time in prayer, allowing the Holy Spirit to speak to our hearts. But hearing isn't enough. We must also yield to His leading, be willing to lay down our own plans, and adjust our path according to His direction. It is through this surrender that we allow God to work through us, shaping our desires to reflect His divine purpose.

As we align our Subconscious Mind with the Mind of Christ and activate the Law of Attraction through NOW faith, we will begin to witness the tangible manifestations of God's promises unfold in our lives. When we embrace God's promise of healing and wholeness, we lay hold of divine health, trusting that by His stripes, we are made well. As we walk in NOW faith, we experience His provision, knowing that Jehovah-Jireh, our provider, supplies all our needs according to His riches in glory. In this alignment, we also find ourselves anchored in a peace that surpasses all understanding (Philippians 4:7), a peace that steadies our hearts despite the storms of life. Finally, we step confidently into the purpose God has called us to, understanding that we are equipped and empowered by His Spirit to fulfill our divine assignment. These are not distant dreams but present realities for those who walk in NOW faith and obedience to His Word.

While the Law of Attraction is indeed powerful, it must always be approached with a heart of humility and submission to God's sovereignty. We must guard against the temptation to use it as a tool for manipulation, trying to force outcomes that are outside of God's will. This law is not meant for self-serving purposes or to manipulate the universe into granting our every desire. Likewise, we must resist the pull of materialism, focusing solely on earthly gains at the expense of eternal treasures. Our pursuit must be for things of lasting value, those aligned with God's kingdom, not merely the temporary riches of this world. Above all, we must never forget the supremacy of God's plans over our own. As Isaiah 55:8-9 reminds us, His thoughts are higher than our thoughts, and His ways are higher than our ways. The true power of the Law of Attraction is found in aligning ourselves with His will, trusting in His sovereignty to guide our desires and bring about the best for our lives.

Embracing the Law of Attraction is not just about achieving immediate results; it's a journey of spiritual growth and transformation. It's a process of becoming more like Christ, continually renewing our minds, and stepping into the fullness of the potential God has placed within us. Along the way, we must cultivate patience, understanding that not every manifestation happens instantly. We trust in God's perfect timing, knowing that He is always working behind the scenes. Resilience is key—staying steadfast in NOW faith even when circumstances appear to contradict what we are believing for. NOW faith doesn't waver in the face of adversity; it grows stronger. And through it all, we must find joy in the journey, knowing with unwavering confidence that God is orchestrating everything for our good, as Romans 8:28 reminds us. Each step in this journey draws us closer to Him, and that is where true fulfillment is found.

The Law of Attraction, grounded in biblical truth, is a divine tool that enables us to live with abundance and purpose. By aligning our Subconscious Mind with the Mind of Christ, breaking free from negative strongholds, and exercising NOW faith, we open the door to God's blessings. As Ephesians 3:20 reminds us, *"God is able to do "exceedingly abundantly above all that we ask or think, according to the power that works in us."*

To fully embrace this truth, we must first commit to renewing our minds daily, immersing ourselves in the life-giving power of God's Word, allowing it to wash over our thoughts, cleanse our perceptions, and transform our inner dialogue. As we align our hearts with His will, we learn to seek His purpose above our own fleeting desires, trusting that His plan far exceeds anything we could ever imagine for ourselves. Walking in NOW faith, we move boldly in the assurance of His promises, stepping out not with hesitation but with a confidence rooted in the knowledge that God is faithful and His Word never returns void. When we operate in this way—mind renewed, heart aligned, and faith activated—we not only experience a transformation in our own lives but become living vessels of His grace, radiating His glory and impacting those around us in ways that echo throughout eternity.

| 6 |

Death of Vanity & Ego-Tapping into God's Blueprint

L earn how overcoming the traps of ego and vanity will unlock divine alignment and reveal God's perfect plan for your life and success.

On the path to success and growth, two formidable obstacles often stand in our way: vanity and ego. These subtle yet pervasive forces can hinder our connection with God, cloud our judgment, and prevent us from realizing the fullness of His purpose for our lives. To tap into our true spiritual power, we must recognize and overcome these barriers, aligning ourselves completely to the will of God.

God's Word is the fountainhead of all wisdom, ideas, inspiration, concepts, technology, learning, teaching, theories, and information. Every revelation and innovation originate from Him. As James 1:17 (NIV) reminds us, *"Every good and perfect gift is from above, coming down from the Father of the heavenly lights."* When we acknowledge God as the ultimate source, we position ourselves to receive His guidance and blessings.

Understanding the interplay between the Conscious and Subconscious Minds is crucial in overcoming vanity and ego. The Subconscious Mind does exactly what the Conscious Mind instructs it to do.

It is like fertile soil that brings forth the seeds sown into it. When we consciously focus on God and His Word, our subconscious aligns with His will, enabling us to manifest His purpose in our lives.

The Wonderful Counselor—flows through everyone who invites Him in. His knowledge is unlimited and all abounding; nothing is impossible for Him. Isaiah 9:6 refers to Him as *"Wonderful Counselor, Mighty God, Everlasting Father, Prince of Peace."* His dominant characteristic is creating frequency-correct images back to the yielded spirit of man. Since He holds all knowledge, substance, and power, the primary action of our Mighty God is to create.

Yet, as this revelation is poured out upon humanity, an old adversary reappears—vanity. Quickly, the gifts of revelation, creativity, and wisdom are attributed to human ingenuity rather than to their true source: God. The result is a dangerous path where the organized thinking of man's ego begins to attract like-minded thinking from the universe. Before long, humanity "thinks" itself into independence from its Creator—attempting, once again, to outsmart God.

"Now the whole world had one language and a common speech. As people moved eastward, they found a plain in Shinar and settled there. They said to each other, "Come, let's make bricks and bake them thoroughly."
They used brick instead of stone, and tar for mortar. Then they said, "Come, let us build ourselves a city, with a tower that reaches to the heavens, so that we may make a name for ourselves; otherwise we will be scattered over the face of the whole earth." But the Lord came down to see the city and the tower the people were building. The Lord said, "If as one people speaking the same language they have begun to do this, then nothing they plan to do will be impossible for them. Come, let us go down and confuse their language so they will not understand each other."
(Genesis 11:1-9 NIV)

This is the age-old story of humanity. As we receive the brilliance of divine revelation, vanity creeps in, leading us to believe that the knowledge, ideas, and innovations are of our own making. This illusion of independence marks the beginning of a spiritual decline. As individuals "think" themselves into separation from God, they embark on a path that distances them from true wisdom and purpose. Proverbs 16:18 (NKJV) warns, *"Pride goes before destruction, and a haughty spirit before a fall."* Man begins to believe that he is self-sufficient, needing nothing beyond his own intellect and strength. Thus begins the fall of another generation—proud, self-reliant, the "go-getter" he is called, and ultimately disconnected from the true source of wisdom.

Vanity and ego are deceptive. Once birthed, they do not like to share credit or acknowledge their origin. Instead, these forces work hard to ensure that we claim credit for what God has provided. These are the violent, wise thinkers always looking for a "secret" source, a pot of gold in which they may claim was created by their own mastery of alchemy. They loot the treasures of the Kingdom of Heaven God so freely gives, not as givers or sharers, but as thieves who raid for their own glory. They seek to be praised for their supposed genius, constantly attempting to reinvent the wheel and claim mastery over creation itself. As the Apostle Paul wrote in Romans 1:21-22 (TLB):

"Yes, they knew about him all right, but they wouldn't admit it or worship him or even thank him for all his daily care. And after a while they began to think up silly ideas of what God was like and what he wanted them to do. The result was that their foolish minds became dark and confused. Claiming themselves to be wise without God, they became utter fools instead."

This warning is clear: those who refuse to acknowledge God as the source of all wisdom, those who seek to place themselves at the center of creation, will fall into foolishness. This pattern repeats throughout history. Humanity becomes self-absorbed, inflating its ego until it is too late, realizing that it is disconnected from the life-giving source—God Himself.

Vanity and ego often creep into our lives subtly. It begins with small successes, moments when we experience the fruits of God's favor and revelation. Instead of giving glory to God, we start believing that we are responsible for the success. This is where the downward spiral begins. The ego begins to crave recognition, validation, and applause. We begin to hunger for the acknowledgment of others rather than the quiet assurance that comes from walking in alignment with God's will.

"Steve Jobs, famously known for his "reality distortion field" way of viewing and "willing" the physical things and circumstances around him, used this power unsuccessfully against his round-1 bout with his early detection of cancer. His wife called his "magical thinking" his assumption that he could "will" things to be as he wanted. Cancer, for him did not work that way."

*(**Steven Jobs** by Walter Isaacson)*

The ego thrives on a sense of superiority. It demands recognition as the master of its domain, separating itself from God and those around it. It becomes the "go-getter"—driven by the pursuit of personal achievement, power, and fame. However, as much as vanity and ego seek to elevate the individual, they are destined for failure. The self-driven life ultimately collapses under the weight of its own pride.

Here are a few additional real-life examples of leaders whose inability to overcome ego and vanity impacted their careers and organizations:

1. Adam Neumann – Former CEO of WeWork
Adam Neumann co-founded WeWork in 2010, and the company quickly grew into a global leader in coworking spaces, at one point

valued at nearly $47 billion. However, Neumann's leadership style and personal behavior raised concerns.

Ego and Vanity:

- Grandiose Vision: Neumann portrayed himself not just as a business leader but as a visionary set to "elevate the world's consciousness." This inflated sense of self led to overambitious expansion plans that outpaced the company's financial reality.
- Personal Profiteering: He made several self-dealing transactions, such as trademarking the word "We" and then selling it back to the company for $5.9 million.
- Extravagant Lifestyle: Neumann was known for lavish spending, including private jets and luxury accommodations, funded by the company.

Fate:

- Failed IPO: In 2019, WeWork's attempt to go public unraveled as investors scrutinized the company's finances and Neumann's leadership.
- Loss of Confidence: Major investors lost faith due to corporate governance issues and Neumann's erratic behavior.
- Resignation: He was forced to step down as CEO and gave up majority voting control.
- Company Valuation Plunged: WeWork's valuation dropped dramatically, leading to massive layoffs and financial losses.

Neumann's inability to temper his ego and align his leadership with sustainable business practices led to personal downfall and jeopardized the company's future.

2. Elizabeth Holmes – Founder and Former CEO of Theranos

Elizabeth Holmes founded Theranos in 2003, a biotech startup that claimed to revolutionize blood testing with a device that could run numerous tests on just a tiny blood sample.

Ego and Vanity:

- Cult of Personality: Holmes fashioned herself after Steve Jobs, adopting his signature black turtleneck and projecting an image of a revolutionary innovator.
- Secrecy Over Transparency: She avoided peer reviews and kept the technology under wraps, insisting on blind trust in her vision.
- Overpromising: Made bold claims about the capabilities of Theranos's technology without scientific validation.

Fate:

- Exposure of Fraud: Investigative journalism revealed that the technology didn't work as advertised, and the company was using standard machines from other manufacturers to run tests.
- Legal Consequences: Holmes was charged with multiple counts of fraud against investors and patients.
- Conviction: In 2022, she was found guilty on several counts of wire fraud and conspiracy.
- Reputation Ruined: Once hailed as the youngest self-made female billionaire, she became a cautionary tale of deceit in Silicon Valley.

Holmes's vanity and desire for fame led her to prioritize her image over ethical responsibilities, resulting in legal repercussions and the collapse of her company.

3. Travis Kalanick – Co-founder and Former CEO of Uber

Travis Kalanick co-founded Uber in 2009, disrupting the transportation industry with ride-sharing services that became globally dominant.

Ego and Vanity:

- Aggressive Expansion: Kalanick pushed for rapid growth often without regard for local regulations, leading to legal challenges worldwide.
- Toxic Culture: Under his leadership, Uber faced numerous allegations of fostering a toxic work environment, including sexual harassment and discrimination.
- Confrontational Behavior: A notable incident involved a video of Kalanick arguing with an Uber driver over falling fares, showcasing a lack of empathy.

Fate:

- Investor Pressure: In 2017, following multiple scandals, major investors demanded his resignation to protect the company's reputation.
- Resignation: Kalanick stepped down as CEO but remained on the board for some time.
- Cultural Overhaul: Uber initiated significant changes to address workplace culture and ethical practices under new leadership.

Kalanick's failure to check his ego and address internal issues harmed Uber's public image and led to his ousting, highlighting the need for responsible leadership.

These examples illustrate how vanity and ego can lead to a leader's downfall:

- Short-Term Success vs. Long-Term Sustainability: While ego-driven strategies might yield immediate results, they often lack the foundation for enduring success.
- Ethical Oversight: Ignoring ethical considerations for personal ambition can result in legal issues and loss of trust.
- Cultural Impact: Leaders set the tone for organizational culture; unchecked ego can foster toxic environments that stifle growth and innovation.

Overcoming vanity and ego is crucial for sustainable leadership. By practicing humility, acknowledging the contributions of others, and aligning with ethical principles, leaders can foster positive growth and fulfill a greater purpose beyond personal accolades.

These real-life cases serve as cautionary tales about the perils of separation from God and allowing ego and vanity to overshadow sound judgment and ethical responsibility. They underscore the importance of aligning leadership with integrity, accountability, and a commitment to serving the greater good.

This separation from God is not merely a philosophical or emotional distance; it disrupts the very spiritual laws that govern our existence. The Conscious Mind of man, driven by ego, attempts to shape the world through willpower, control, and manipulation. It operates independently of God, seeking to create without acknowledging the divine source that fuels all creation. Yet, it is only through the alignment of the Subconscious Mind with the Spirit of God that true creation can occur.

When the Subconscious Mind is yielded to God, the spirit within us aligns with His will. As we think, imagine, and speak, the Spirit of Creation responds, forming the image back to us based on what we project into Him through prayer. We become "Matter Miners," extracting the manifest reality of God's promises through NOW faith and willing submission to His immutable laws.

However, when the Conscious Mind—dominated by vanity and ego—seeks to create independently, it disrupts this flow. The ego-driven mind lacks the spiritual power and frequency to produce lasting results. It strives but fails, for it is disconnected from the true source of creation. The ego, in its pursuit of glory, constructs a false sense of self-sufficiency. It positions itself as the creator and sustainer of its success, all the while drifting further from the life-giving Spirit of Wonderful Counselor.

One of the most dangerous manifestations of vanity and ego is the "go-getter" mentality—the belief that through sheer determination, hard work, and self-reliance, one can accomplish anything. While ambition and drive are not inherently wrong, when they are rooted in the ego rather than submission to God's will, they lead to spiritual emptiness.

The "go-getter" seeks to claim all the keys available without true guidance. I'm reminded, by the "go-getter", of the movie Avengers, where Thanos sought all six of the Infinity Stones so he could control time. Thanos believed that by collecting all the stones, he could control time and bend the universe to his will. His pursuit of absolute power was driven by a desire to achieve his own vision of balance, detached from the source of all wisdom—God. In the same way, the ego-driven go-getter strives to gather the keys to success, control, and influence. However, the key to true spiritual power is not found in self-reliance but in submission to God's will.

Christ said He would give us the keys to the kingdom—not so we could pursue our own agendas, but so that we could unlock the mysteries of heaven in alignment with His purpose. Ego blinds us to the true nature of these keys, making us believe we must seize them through personal effort rather than receiving them as divine gifts.

The only way to overcome the vanity and ego that limit our success and growth is through humility and surrender. We must consciously acknowledge that all wisdom, all creativity, and all power originate from God. As we do, we free ourselves from the bondage of self-reliance and open ourselves to the limitless possibilities of life in alignment with God's will.

Humility is not self-deprecation; it is a recognition that we are vessels of God's grace, not the source of it. When we humble ourselves before God, we allow His Spirit to work through us, manifesting His glory in our lives. Ego-driven accomplishments pale in comparison to what God can do through a heart that is fully surrendered to Him. By surrendering our will to God's, we move from a place of striving to a place of rest. We no longer need to "go-get" because we are operating under the divine law of attraction—where God brings forth the Matter and His promises in our lives as we align with His purpose. In this place of surrender, we unlock the true power of the Spirit of Creation, allowing us to manifest God's will on earth as it is in heaven.

To access your true spiritual power, you must overcome vanity and ego. These forces, though subtle, separate us from God's creative flow and prevent us from fulfilling our highest potential. By acknowledging God as the source of all wisdom and submitting to His will, you free yourself from the burdens of self-reliance and unlock the infinite possibilities He offers. To overcome vanity and ego, we must realign our conscious mind with God's will.

The journey to fully harness the Law of Attraction and live in alignment with God's will begins with intentional steps of spiritual discipline and surrender. These steps are not just about thinking positively or manifesting our desires—they are about positioning ourselves in humility and obedience to God's principles and laws, allowing His power to flow through us. True transformation requires us to let go of self and align with the Mind of Christ, becoming instruments of His grace and power in the world.

The first step in this journey is to embrace humility before God. James 4:10 reminds us, *"Humble yourselves before the Lord, and He will lift you up."* Every gift, talent, and opportunity we possess comes from Him, not from our own efforts. Humility is the foundation that opens the door to divine guidance and empowerment. When we acknowledge our dependence on God, we release the grip of pride and ego, making room for His Spirit to move freely in our lives. It is only in this posture of humility that we can be truly lifted to the heights of success He has planned for us.

Next, we must renew our minds with God's Word. Romans 12:2 challenges us to break free from the world's patterns and be transformed by renewing our thoughts. The Word of God is the tool that reprograms our minds, aligning our conscious and subconscious thoughts with His truth. Regular meditation on Scripture allows us to diminish the influence of ego and replace it with divine wisdom. This daily renewal sharpens our focus, ensuring that we are not swayed by fleeting desires or worldly distractions, but instead, are rooted in God's eternal truth.

Surrendering control is another key step in this process. Proverbs 3:5-6 instructs us to *"Trust in the Lord with all your heart and lean not on your own understanding."* This means letting go of our need to control every outcome and trusting that God's plan is greater than our own. When we surrender, we invite Him to guide and order our steps and make our paths straight. Trusting His wisdom over our limited understanding allows us to walk in the confidence that He is working all things for our good, even when we can't see the full picture.

To further dismantle the power of ego, we must serve others self-lessly. Jesus Himself modeled servant leadership, reminding us that true greatness comes from serving others (Matthew 20:26-28). When we shift our focus from self-centered pursuits to serving those around us, we align our hearts with God's purpose for humanity. This act of service not only blesses others but also deepens our connection to God, allowing His love to flow through us in powerful ways. It's through service that we truly become like Christ, and in doing so, we dismantle the ego's desire for personal gain.

Finally, we must cultivate gratitude. Gratitude keeps us mindful of our dependence on God and protects us from the corrosive influence of ego. 1 Thessalonians 5:18 calls us to *"Give thanks in all circumstances."* By regularly thanking God for His provision, care, and blessings, we stay grounded in the knowledge that every good thing in our lives is a gift from Him. Gratitude shifts our perspective from what we lack to what we've already been given, allowing us to see the sufficient full-ness of God's grace in every situation. In this attitude of gratitude, we walk in the power of God's will, knowing He is faithful to fulfill His promises.

When we free ourselves from vanity and ego, we position our-selves to grow spiritually and tap into God's greater purpose for our lives. We become vessels through which His love, wisdom, and power flow into the world. Our actions begin to reflect His character, and our lives bear fruit that honors Him. Jesus taught in John 15:8 (NIV), *"This is to my Father's glory, that you bear much fruit, showing yourselves to be my disciples."* By abiding in Him and relinquishing our ego-driven ambitions, we align with our true spiritual power and experience the fullness of joy that comes from walking in His ways.

Overcoming vanity and ego is an ongoing process that requires vigilance and dependence on God. As we submit our Conscious Minds to Him, our Subconscious aligns with His Spirit, enabling us to manifest His will on earth. We move from self-centered striving to God-centered living, experiencing the abundant life He promises.

The journey is not about becoming a "go-getter" but about becoming a surrendered vessel, through whom God's Spirit seated in our heart can flow unhindered. As you align your mind and spirit with His, you will discover the true keys to the kingdom—where nothing is impossible, and every dream aligned with His will can be made manifest.

| 7 |

Crossing the Chasm-Mining the Blueprint of Success

*D*iscover *the powerful shift in accepting the treasures, planted images as a key to bridge the gap of thought – transforming God's immutable dynamic laws into material abundance and prosperity.*

In the pursuit of success, whether in business or personal life, we often find ourselves caught in a great chasm between two worlds: the spiritual realm of beliefs and convictions, and the tangible world of material existence. The challenge lies in bridging this gap—aligning the accepted images of our inner thoughts with our outward actions to achieve success and true abundance.

On one side of the chasm, the Subconscious Mind, seated in the heart, is the wellspring of our deepest beliefs and convictions, the desires of our hearts, the material abundance, the prosperity and success we visualize. Jesus emphasized this when He said, *"A good man out of the good treasure of his heart brings forth good things"* (Matthew 12:35). Our subconscious beliefs shape our reality, influencing the opportunities we attract and the actions we take. To effectively harness the Dynamic Laws that govern the success necessary to cross this abyss, we must first ensure that our Subconscious Mind is in harmony with the downloads received from the Mind of Christ.

This alignment requires introspection and the deliberate uprooting of any strongholds—negative beliefs—that contradict His promises. These strongholds usually manifest as doubts, fears, vain arguments, questionings, or limiting beliefs that hinder our progress. By Mining the Mind of Christ—the ultimate source of wisdom and insight—we tap into a well of infinite potential. As "Matter Miners," we extract the treasures hidden within, turning divine ideas into tangible results.

The Law of Attraction isn't about manipulating circumstances to fulfill selfish desires. It's about aligning our will with God's, allowing His plans to manifest through us. When Jesus taught us to pray, *"Your kingdom come, Your will be done on earth as it is in heaven"* (Matthew 6:10), He was highlighting the importance of syncing our intentions with the Wonderful Counselor. Success, in its truest form, emerges when our goals resonate with God's design for our lives.

NOW Faith is the currency of the Kingdom of Heaven—a powerful force that activates the Dynamic Laws set by God. *"Now faith is the substance of things hoped for, the evidence of things not seen"* (Hebrews 11:1). NOW faith bridges the gap between the invisible and the visible, turning our inner convictions into real-world achievements. It's not blind optimism but a confident assurance in God's faithfulness and the laws He established.

In today's fast-paced world, modern day Sadducees and Pharisees, known as skeptics might say, "Man is a builder and a doer with his hands, and it's foolish to think that success can be achieved by thought alone." Or they might scoff, "If you're serious about your goals, stop daydreaming and go out and get them." Many well-intentioned individuals have been led off the right path by such misguided advice—what has been termed False Evidence Appearing Real.

But consider this: nobody achieves lasting success by merely "going out and getting it." This mindset implies that what we seek belongs to someone else and must be taken. True success comes from creating our own Matter, on the plane of the mind, the conviction that what we desire is already ours. When we cultivate this belief, we're guided along the proper paths and into the right actions that lead to our goals.

Action is essential, but not all action yields results. There's a difference between busywork and purposeful action. False action—efforts not aligned with true thought—won't move a molehill. In contrast, true action, born from aligned thoughts and beliefs, can dissolve mountains. If your thoughts are true and grounded in the Dynamic Laws, your actions will be impeccably guided by the Subconscious Mind fully yielded to the Mind of Christ.

It's crucial to exercise caution when trying to "will" things into existence. Willpower often focuses on overcoming obstacles that may actually be steppingstones placed by God. *"The steps of a good man are ordered by the Lord"* (Psalm 37:23). Pushing against these can lead to unnecessary struggle. Instead, willingly place your trust in the free flow that the Mind of Christ gives when your will is in alignment with His.

Think of successful entrepreneurs and leaders who've seemingly defied odds. Their journeys weren't just about hard work; they involved a deep alignment of belief, purpose, and action. They tapped into Dynamic Laws higher than themselves, often attributing their insights and breakthroughs to a source beyond mere intellect.

Here are several such examples of successful entrepreneurs and leaders who defied the odds by aligning their beliefs, purpose, and actions. Their journeys involved tapping into principles higher than themselves, often attributing their insights and breakthroughs to a source beyond mere intellect. They found harmony between their inner beliefs and the material world while navigating the path to success and abundance.

1. Oprah Winfrey – Media Mogul and Philanthropist

Alignment of Belief, Purpose, and Action:

- Overcoming Adversity: Born into poverty in rural Mississippi, Oprah faced significant challenges, including childhood abuse and discrimination. Despite these hardships, she cultivated a strong sense of self and purpose.
- Spiritual Alignment: Oprah attributes much of her success to her spiritual beliefs and practices. She is a proponent of mindfulness, gratitude, and the Law of Attraction, often discussing these topics on her shows and platforms.
- Purpose-Driven Work: Her career has been dedicated to empowering others, focusing on personal growth, healing, and transformation. She created "The Oprah Winfrey Show" not just as entertainment but as a medium to inspire and uplift.
- Attributing Success Beyond Herself: Oprah frequently acknowledges a higher power guiding her journey. She speaks openly about her faith and the role it plays in her decision-making and success.

Outcome:

- Media Empire: Built a media conglomerate including television shows, a magazine, a radio channel, and the OWN television network.
- Philanthropy: Founded the Oprah Winfrey Leadership Academy for Girls in South Africa and has donated millions to educational causes.

- Global Influence: Recognized as one of the most influential women in the world, Oprah continues to impact lives through her authentic alignment of inner beliefs with outward actions.

2. Howard Schultz – Former CEO of Starbucks
Alignment of Belief, Purpose, and Action:

- Humble Beginnings: Howard Schultz grew up in a poor family in Brooklyn, New York. He was the first in his family to graduate from college.
- Vision Beyond Coffee: Schultz envisioned Starbucks as a "third place" between work and home, a community hub fostering human connection.
- Principle-Centered Leadership: He emphasized ethical business practices, employee welfare, and social responsibility. Starbucks was one of the first companies to offer stock options and healthcare benefits to part-time employees.
- Attributing Success to Higher Principles: Schultz often speaks about servant leadership and the importance of mission-driven business. He believes in balancing profit with social conscience.

Outcome:

- Global Brand Expansion: Under his leadership, Starbucks grew from a small regional chain to a global phenomenon with thousands of stores worldwide.
- Corporate Social Responsibility: Implemented programs for ethical sourcing, environmental stewardship, and community service.
- Legacy of Compassionate Leadership: Schultz's approach has influenced how businesses view the integration of employee well-being and social impact with commercial success.

3. Sara Blakely – Founder of Spanx
Alignment of Belief, Purpose, and Action:

- Turning Setbacks into Opportunities: After failing the LSAT twice and selling fax machines door-to-door, Blakely sought a new direction, driven by a desire to improve women's lives.
- Intuition and Visualization: She credits her success to trusting her gut feelings and practicing visualization techniques. Blakely wrote her goals and envisioned her products helping women worldwide.
- Purpose to Empower: Created Spanx with the mission to help women feel confident. She maintained 100% ownership initially to ensure her vision wasn't compromised.
- Attributing Success Beyond Herself: Blakely often speaks about the role of mindset and the universe in her success. She believes in the Law of Attraction and that her positive intentions attracted opportunities.

Outcome:

- Self-Made Billionaire: Became the youngest self-made female billionaire in 2012.
- Innovative Products: Revolutionized the shapewear industry with a product line that emphasizes comfort and confidence.
- Philanthropy and Mentorship: Founded the Sara Blakely Foundation to support women through education and entrepreneurial training.

4. Tyler Perry – Actor, Director, Producer, and Screenwriter
Alignment of Belief, Purpose, and Action:

- Overcoming Adversity: Tyler Perry grew up in New Orleans in a challenging environment, facing poverty and abuse during his childhood. Despite dropping out of high school, he found solace and expression through writing, using it as a means to process his experiences.

- Faith and Spirituality: Perry attributes much of his resilience and success to his strong Christian faith. He often incorporates themes of redemption, forgiveness, and faith in his work, reflecting his personal journey and beliefs.
- Purpose-Driven Content: He began his career by writing and producing plays that highlighted social issues affecting the African-American community. His signature character, "Madea," became a cultural icon known for her wisdom, humor, and tough love, delivering messages of empowerment and self-worth.
- Attributing Success Beyond Himself: Perry frequently acknowledges God's role in his life, expressing gratitude for the guidance and opportunities he has received. He emphasizes the importance of listening to a higher calling and being obedient to that divine direction.

Outcome:

- Entertainment Empire: Tyler Perry built a multimedia empire, including successful films, television shows, and stage productions that have resonated with diverse audiences. His works have grossed over a billion dollars worldwide.
- Studio Ownership: In 2019, he opened Tyler Perry Studios in Atlanta, Georgia—one of the largest film studios in the United States—making him the first African-American to own a major film studio outright.
- Philanthropy and Community Impact: Perry is known for his generous philanthropy, supporting various causes such as education, homelessness, disaster relief, and assistance to individuals facing personal hardships. He often uses his resources to uplift others, staying true to his mission of empowerment.

These leaders embody the truth that when spiritual convictions are intertwined with material pursuits, success takes on a profound and lasting impact. By aligning their God-given talents with a higher purpose, they not only achieved extraordinary personal success but also became beacons of hope and inspiration for countless others. Their lives serve as living examples of how one can walk in both divine purpose and material abundance without losing sight of the mission. This is not just about wealth accumulation; it's about living a life of meaningful contribution, rooted in principles that transcend personal ambition.

First and foremost, these leaders achieved inner alignment, cultivating a deep connection with their purpose through regular introspection, NOW faith practices, and spiritual disciplines. Whether through prayer, meditation, or time spent in quiet reflection, they consistently sought guidance beyond themselves, keeping their spirits in tune with God's will. This inner alignment allowed them to make decisions from a place of clarity and conviction, ensuring their pursuits were not only successful but also meaningful. They understood that success flows first from being aligned with a higher calling and that their actions were a reflection of their spiritual values.

Secondly, their ventures were driven by altruistic purpose over profit. These leaders didn't just chase financial gain or recognition. Instead, they committed to serving and uplifting others through their businesses, organizations, or missions. They knew that their accomplishments were not simply the result of intellectual prowess but were inspired by laws rooted in something greater than themselves. As a result, their legacies extended far beyond personal wealth, leaving a lasting positive impact on their communities, industries, and cultural narratives. Through this divine alignment and dedication to purpose, they became conduits of grace, hope, and transformation for others.

In the pantheon of leaders and entrepreneurs are the many incredible success stories of those who have defied the odds through aligning their beliefs and actions with a higher calling, one stands out to me on a deeply personal level—my wife, **Shyla Janon'ne Jacobs**—a woman who embodies the power of resilience, creativity, and divine alignment. Known affectionately as "Ten Talents," Shyla has yielded her God-given gifts into a life of extraordinary personal success, not only in the entertainment industry but also in her ministry, touching countless lives with her story of triumph. While the world recognizes names like Tyler Perry, Oprah Winfrey, Howard Schultz, and Sara Blakely for their monumental achievements, Shyla stands among them, shining even brighter in my eyes as a beacon of hope, strength, and unwavering faith.

Shyla at 17-years old as Member of Ike Turner Revue 1991-1994 (Far Right)

Island Records

Though noticeably set apart and peculiar from a young age, Shyla's journey has been one marked by many challenges. Like a wildflower blooming in adversity, she endured emotional and sexual abuse, suffered with mental health issues and alcoholism, while her giftings and talents yet emerged, serving as an outlet and would eventually make evident her calling. Along with the countless dreams and visions she would have that seemed to hold messages from heaven, she had inclinations towards the arts. From singing and writing, to acting and doing impressions of entertainers like Robin Leach and Jean Stapleton' s All in the Family character "Edith Bunker", she dazzled others with her wit and charm.

At just 17, Shyla had the rare opportunity to tour with Ike Turner, serving as an Ikette for the legendary Ike Turner Review from 1991 to 1994. Her voice was so captivating that Ike envisioned her as his "new Tina," a role she carried with discipline and dedication.

Touring with Ike taught her valuable lessons about the grit and perseverance needed to pursue any dream, as well as the importance of integrity in an industry that can be filled with half-truths and manipulation. But God had greater plans for her beyond this chapter. Her path would take her through multiple facets of the entertainment world, including a brief stint as the third singer for the female R&B group Nuttin' Nyce and a recording deal with Solar Music Group. She has written, arranged, and recorded over 15 original songs, including hits like "Love Sick", "Around", "Goin' Down", "Let Love Reign", "Garden", and "I Can".

She went on to write, produce, direct, act, and sing in her own live stage play, Surrender ROW. A powerful narrative of redemption and faith that resonates with both believers and those searching for hope. The accompanying soundtrack, also written and performed by Shyla, captures the depth of her journey—every note a testament to her transformation through faith.

In addition to her artistic talents, Shyla is a deeply anointed vessel of God's word. At church, she doesn't just sing—she ministers through musical preaching, exhortation, and a prophetic flow. Her presence is a blessing, her voice a healing balm that touches hearts, bringing people to repentance, restoring faith and joy.

Additionally, she authored and published "Brite Saves the Day", an inspirational children's book with lessons about God's love, the acceptance of self and others, bullying and forgiveness. Not content to stop there, Shyla founded the Divine Sisterhood, a ministry that empowers women to navigate the many roles they hold in life—whether as wives, mothers, or business owners—while staying rooted in their faith. She has hosted her own radio show, podcast, and YouTube channel, always using her gifts to bring joy, laughter, and spiritual upliftment to her audience.

She has not only achieved extraordinary personal success but also serves as a living example of resilience, creativity, and divine fulfillment. Through her life and work, her light shines even brighter—becoming a woman whose accomplishments would make even the most well-known leaders pale in comparison.

These examples serve as inspiration for anyone seeking to navigate the path to success and abundance. They demonstrate that success is not solely the result of hard work and intellect but also of aligning oneself with higher principles and purposes.

Bridging the spiritual and material worlds isn't about abandoning practical efforts or dismissing the importance of action. Rather, it's about ensuring that your actions are fueled by aligned thoughts and a clear purpose rooted in divine wisdom. It's about recognizing that success isn't a zero-sum game but an abundant field where everyone can thrive when connected to the right source.

So how do you apply this in your life? Start by examining your beliefs about success, wealth, and your own capabilities. Are there limiting beliefs, strongholds, holding you back? Replace them with truths drawn from the Mind of Christ. Meditate on scriptures that affirm your potential and God's plans for you. *"For I know the plans I have for you,"* declares the Lord, *"plans to prosper you and not to harm you, plans to give you hope and a future"* (Jeremiah 29:11).

Next, align your goals with a higher purpose. Ask yourself how your ambitions serve not just you but also contribute positively to others. When your objectives align with God's will, you position yourself to receive His guidance and favor.

Finally, take inspired action. Don't just act for the sake of being busy. Seek direction from the Everlasting Father, and let the Wonderful Counselor guide your steps. This doesn't mean there won't be challenges, but you'll face them with confidence, knowing you're on the right path.

In bridging the gap between your inner beliefs and the material world, you harness the Dynamic Laws God put in place. You move from merely chasing success to attracting it, from striving to thriving. Your life becomes a testament to what's possible when you align with divine principles—impacting not just yourself but inspiring those around you.

Remember, success isn't just about what you achieve but who you become in the process. By Mining the Mind of Christ and aligning with God's Dynamic Laws, you unlock the door to true abundance and fulfillment.

Heavenly Father, thank You for the dynamic laws You've established, guiding us toward success and abundance. Help us to align our thoughts and beliefs with Your truth, yielding our Subconscious Minds to the Mind of Christ. May we bridge the gap between our inner convictions and our actions, living lives that reflect Your purpose and bring glory to Your name. In Jesus' name, we pray. Amen.

| 8 |

Rebellion to Ruin-Why Transgression Blocks Success

*R*ebellion *against set authority is more than disobedience—it's a road-block to everything you're meant to achieve. Learn from the consequences of rebellion as shown in King Saul's life, and explore the power of submission and observing divine order leads to personal breakthrough and prosperity.*

In the grand design of life, authority is the thread that holds both the fabric of society and our spiritual walk together. It's the immutable divine order God set in place to bring structure, purpose, and peace to our existence. Whether it's the laws of a nation or the dynamic spiritual laws that guide our hearts, aligning ourselves under this authority is not just about obedience—it's about unlocking the fullness of our destiny. But let's be honest—the spirit of rebellion is always lurking, tempting us to step outside these boundaries. And while rebellion might seem liberating in the moment, it brings with it consequences that can throw us off course and block the blessings God intends for our lives.

The danger in exercising our will to attain specific things lies in the subtle trap of ego. When we become consumed with our desires, we risk isolating ourselves from the divine power that we've invoked through faith. On one hand, we call upon this power with NOW faith and conviction; on the other, by imposing our will, we may inadvertently deny it or redirect it away from its intended purpose.

Consequently, all effort should be aimed at gaining guidance through attunement with the Mind of Christ. This alignment requires complete NOW faith and trust that the infinite power of the Wonderful Counselor will manifest the image of our NOW faith. Any subsequent attempt to manipulate circumstances through our own will becomes an imposition on God's will—a rebellion against divine order.

Consider the story of King Saul from the Scriptures. Anointed by God as the first king of Israel, Saul started his reign with humility and promise. However, his disobedience and tendency to act on his own will led to his downfall. In 1 Samuel 15:22-23 (NIV), the prophet Samuel confronts Saul, saying:

"Does the Lord delight in burnt offerings and sacrifices as much as in obeying the Lord? To obey is better than sacrifice... For rebellion is like the sin of divination, and arrogance like the evil of idolatry."

Saul's rebellion against divine authority cost him his kingdom. His story serves as a cautionary tale about the consequences of prioritizing personal will over God's directives.

Bad luck doesn't overtake you; you create it. Success isn't the result of hard work; it is the result of right thoughts seeds of right thinking. God always forgives us; we are punished as a result of a transgression of a Dynamic Law such as the "effect of the cause" we put in motion when we committed the inequity. Being forgiven doesn't mute any Dynamic Laws that govern nature and justly judge all who observe or transgress.

The Dynamic Law of Cause and Effect. You throw a stone in a lake, the visible effect is the ripple, the invisible effect is the fish the stone pinned down at the bottom that you are trying to catch to eat. Now you're hungry. God provided the lake and your fish for dinner. You threw stones, even though you knew better. God established Dynamic Laws that naturally enforce any violation or transgression on our part. In that regard, we actually punish ourselves, but often easily accept the fiery darts of weed seeds blaming God from the unseen spiritual enemy - the accuser of the brethren.

Sowing and reaping, or stated another way, Seed Time and Harvest Time, is the basis for all Cause-and-Effect Dynamic Laws. Put the seed of failure in the Subconscious Mind and it will develop failure for you. Put the seed of rebellion, disobedience and unhappiness in the Subconscious Mind and it will develop destructive behavior, contempt for justice, and a deep sense of pessimism for you.

On January 6, 2021, a significant event unfolded in the United States that serves as a contemporary illustration of the consequences of rebellion against established authority. The FBI estimates that between 2,000 and 2,500 individuals unlawfully entered the U.S. Capitol Building during a joint session of Congress convened to certify the results of the 2020 presidential election. This assembly represents a cornerstone of the nation's democratic process, a ritual that upholds the peaceful transition of power.

The actions of these individuals led to confrontations with law enforcement, resulting in injuries to Capitol Police officers and others. Tragically, lives were lost, and the Capitol—a symbol of democratic governance—suffered vandalism and destruction. Offices of public officials, including then-House Speaker Nancy Pelosi and other members of Congress, were breached and damaged. The scenes of chaos and disorder were broadcast worldwide, sending shockwaves through the global community.

This event not only disrupted a fundamental democratic process but also had profound earthly and spiritual consequences. On an earthly level, the immediate aftermath included arrests, legal prosecutions, and a heightened sense of division within the nation. The incident prompted widespread reflection on the state of civic discourse, the impact of misinformation, and the responsibilities inherent in exercising freedoms.

From a spiritual perspective, the events of that day highlight the ramifications of rebelling against established authority—a concept deeply rooted in divine order. Scripture teaches us about the importance of respecting authority as part of God's design for societal harmony. In Romans 13:1-2 (NIV), the Apostle Paul writes:

"Let everyone be subject to the governing authorities, for there is no authority except that which God has established. The authorities that exist have been established by God. Consequently, whoever rebels against the authority is rebelling against what God has instituted."

By defying lawful authority, the participants in the Capitol breach stepped out of alignment with both societal and spiritual laws. Their actions serve as a modern embodiment of the dangers outlined in authority, rebellion, and divine order. The rebellion not only led to immediate chaos but also sowed seeds of mistrust and discord that can hinder a nation's unity and spiritual well-being.

The spiritual consequences extend beyond the individuals involved. Such acts of rebellion can disrupt the collective conscience of a community, leading to a ripple effect of fear, anger, and disillusionment. They challenge the moral fabric of society, prompting introspection about the values and principles that guide us.

This event underscores the critical importance of aligning our actions with both earthly laws and divine directives. It reminds us that exercising our will without regard for established authority can lead to destructive outcomes. As we discussed earlier, the proper use of will is in choosing thoughts and actions that promote harmony, respect, and alignment with the Mind of Christ.

In reflecting on January 6, we are called to examine our own attitudes toward authority. Are we exercising discernment and aligning our will with a higher purpose? Or are we allowing ego and personal agendas to drive actions that contribute to disorder and strife?

The consequences faced by those involved in the Capitol breach serve as a warning narrative. Legal repercussions, damaged reputations, and the burden of contributing to a painful chapter in history are tangible outcomes of their rebellion. Spiritually, they may face inner turmoil and a disconnection from the peace that comes with living in alignment with divine order.

This moment calls us to pause and reflect, offering a unique opportunity for collective healing and a recommitment to the principles that foster unity, respect, and order. It beckons us to respect established authority, recognizing that laws and institutions are not arbitrary but exist to maintain order and serve the greater good. Whether we like it or not, these systems are in place for a reason, to guide us and protect the structure of society. When we respect authority, we are not just obeying human institutions; we are honoring the very fabric that holds our world together.

Yet, this goes deeper than earthly institutions. It requires us to align with divine order, understanding that rebellion against rightful authority is not just civil disobedience, but a direct challenge to God's design for harmony. Rebellion breeds chaos, but when we channel our passions and convictions into constructive action, we build up instead of tearing down. We need to be people who seek to promote healing and unity by bridging divides through empathy, honest dialogue, and a shared commitment to higher principles. In doing so, we move beyond division and enter into a place where we become agents of peace and transformation.

In the broader context of our lives, the lessons from this event encourage us to examine how we respond to authority in various settings—be it in our workplaces, communities, or personal relationships. By aligning our will with both earthly and divine authority, we navigate the path of righteousness and contribute to a more harmonious world. As we move forward, let us remember the words from 1 Peter 2:13-17 (NIV):

"Submit yourselves for the Lord's sake to every human authority... Live as free people, but do not use your freedom as a cover-up for evil; live as God's slaves. Show proper respect to everyone, love the family of believers, fear God, honor the emperor."

By embracing this scriptural guidance, we position ourselves to receive the blessings that come from obedience and to play our part in upholding the divine order that sustains both our spiritual journey and societal well-being.

You are not bigger than God. You've been blessed to be a little "g", a partner, in His eternal plan. Attempting to will against this plan not only abrogates it but also sets the divine power moving in a different, often detrimental, direction. Directing your will toward manipulating the physical world without divine guidance avails nothing and ultimately defeats you. This realization might prompt the question: "What is my own will to be used for, then?" The answer may surprise you. There is one essential area where you must exercise your will—your choice of thoughts. Herein lies the foundation of the Dynamic Law of Attraction. <u>Whatever you will to think, you think</u>.

The type of thoughts you choose automatically attracts corresponding Matter into your life.

As the Apostle Paul advises:

"Finally, brethren, whatsoever things are true, whatsoever things are honest, whatsoever things are just, whatsoever things are pure, whatsoever things are lovely, whatsoever things are of good report; if there be any virtue, and if there be any praise, think on these things."
(Philippians 4:8 KJV)

By exercising your will to focus on these positive and virtuous thoughts, you align yourself with divine authority and open the channels for God's power to flow through you.

Rebellion isn't merely an act of defiance against earthly systems; it's a spiritual posture that resists divine order. When we rebel, we step out of alignment with God's protection and provision. This misalignment can manifest as chaos, confusion, and stagnation in various areas of our lives, just as we witnessed on January 6, 2021.

The Israelites wandered in the wilderness for forty years due to their rebellious nature. Despite witnessing miraculous signs and wonders, they allowed doubt and disobedience to dictate their actions. Their journey illustrates how rebellion prolongs our struggles and delays the fulfillment of God's promises.

The first step toward aligning with both spiritual and earthly authority is to submit your will to God. This requires a deep acknowledgment that His plans and purposes are far greater than our own limited understanding. Proverbs 3:5-6 reminds us to "Trust in the Lord with all your heart and lean not on your own understanding." This is more than a casual surrender; it's about actively submitting every area of your life—your decisions, desires, and ambitions—to the sovereignty of God. When we align our will with His, the paths we are meant to walk become clear, and God Himself will direct our steps. The choice to submit is not a sign of weakness, but of wisdom, for it acknowledges that God's perspective is infinite while ours remains finite.

Next, we must learn to respect earthly authorities as an extension of divine order. Romans 13:1 teaches that "there is no authority except that which God has established." When we submit to the laws and institutions placed over us, we are not merely obeying human leaders—we are honoring the structure that God has set in place. This respect for earthly authority reflects our deeper respect for God's rule over the universe. Rebellion, in contrast, disrupts the divine flow and brings chaos into our lives. It is essential to remember that God works through the systems He has allowed, and by respecting them, we are cooperating with His greater plan.

Another vital component of alignment is to guard your thoughts and seek divine guidance. Our thoughts are the seeds that shape our reality, and we must exercise our will to focus on what is in harmony with God's Word. The battle begins in the mind, where we must intentionally reject lies and negativity and cultivate a mindset that aligns with divine purpose. To do this effectively, we must attune ourselves to the Mind of Christ, ensuring that every action we take is guided by His wisdom, not our own ego. This is where humility comes in—understanding that we are participants in God's grand design, not the orchestrators. Humility keeps us teachable and open to correction, both of which are essential for growth and aligning with the higher order God has ordained.

Obedience is the antidote to rebellion. It positions us under God's covering, where His favor and blessings flow freely. Obedience isn't about blind submission; it's about trusting that God's commands are designed for our ultimate good.

Jesus exemplified perfect obedience. In the Garden of Gethsemane, facing the imminent crucifixion, He prayed, *"Father, if You are willing, take this cup from Me; yet not My will, but Yours be done"* (Luke 22:42 NIV). His submission to the Father's will, despite personal anguish, resulted in the salvation of humanity.

God has granted us free will—not to rebel against Him, but to choose Him willingly. Our will is best utilized in choosing to align our thoughts and actions with His purpose. By consciously deciding to focus on thoughts that are true, noble, and pure, we exercise our will in a way that honors God and propels us toward our destiny.

Consider the analogy of a sailor adjusting the sails. The wind represents God's power and direction. While we cannot control the wind, we can adjust our sails—our thoughts and attitudes—to harness its power effectively. Misaligned sails result in missed opportunities and stagnation, but properly adjusted sails allow us to move forward with grace and speed.

When we stubbornly insist on our own way, ignoring the divine guidance that's meant to lead us, we don't just delay our progress—we invite consequences that can derail our purpose entirely. A misaligned will places us outside the flow of God's perfect plan, and the result is often frustration. Constant obstacles and setbacks are not just random occurrences; they may be signs that we are pushing against the grain of God's design for our lives. This rebellion not only creates friction but also leads to isolation, distancing us from the very people and divine connections meant to support us on our journey. Worse yet, by clinging to our own agenda, we risk missing the blessings that flow from obedience—blessings that were ready to manifest the moment we surrendered to His will. Ultimately, when we stray from alignment with God's order, we forfeit the abundance, peace, and progress that come from walking in harmony with His plan.

Aligning with the Mind of Christ doesn't mean relinquishing ambition or desire; it means submitting them to God's will. Psalm 37:4 (NIV) encourages us, *"Take delight in the Lord, and He will give you the desires of your heart."* When our desires align with His, we find fulfillment beyond what we could achieve on our own.

The first step toward aligning your will with God's is to make daily surrender a practice. Each morning, before stepping into the demands of the day, offer your plans to God. This isn't just a fleeting prayer but a conscious act of submission, asking for His guidance and staying open to His leading in every decision, big or small. Surrender isn't passive; it's actively seeking God's direction and choosing to walk in step with His will. As you do this, it's essential to meditate on Scripture, allowing His Word to shape and renew your mind. God's Word is the anchor that aligns your thoughts with His truth, keeping you grounded when the world around you tries to pull you off course. Immerse yourself in it, and you'll find that your thinking begins to shift, aligning more with the wisdom of Christ.

To stay aligned, you must also practice mindfulness. Be aware of your thoughts and intentions throughout the day, recognizing when negativity or rebellion starts to creep in. When it does, make the conscious choice to replace those thoughts with ones that are centered on God and His promises. Surround yourself with a community that reinforces this alignment by seeking wise counsel from mentors and peers who respect divine authority and walk in obedience themselves. Their godly advice can help keep you accountable and focused. Finally, cultivate gratitude in your daily life. Gratitude humbles the heart and fosters a spirit of obedience, reminding you of the blessings that flow from a surrendered will. Focusing on what God has already done keeps you in a state of thankfulness and trust, making it easier to follow His lead.

Authority, both spiritual and earthly, is established for our benefit. Rebellion may offer the illusion of freedom, but it ultimately leads to bondage. By understanding the consequences of misdirected will and choosing to align with divine order, we tap into a power far greater than ourselves.

Remember, the most significant exercise of your will is in choosing your thoughts. As you align your mind with the Mind of Christ, you position yourself to receive guidance, wisdom, and favor. Embrace the Dynamic Law that *"whatsoever you will to think, you think,"* and let your thoughts be a conduit for God's transformative power in your life.

Heavenly Father, we thank You for the authority You've established in our lives. Help us to recognize and respect both spiritual and earthly authorities. Grant us the humility to submit our wills to Yours, and guide our thoughts to align with Your truth. May we embrace Your divine order, knowing that obedience to You leads to true freedom and fulfillment. In Jesus' name, we pray. Amen.

| 9 |

Beyond the Go-Getter-Law of Love, Honor & Exchange

L earn the divine secrets of aligning with God's will by honoring others, living with integrity, and how embracing love, unlocks the pathway to lasting abundance.

In the grand design of life, we are participants in a dynamic interplay of actions and reactions, giving and receiving, sowing and reaping. At the heart of this interplay lies the Law of Mutual Exchange, a divine principle that governs the flow of blessings, opportunities, and relationships in our lives. This law operates on the foundations of integrity, honor, and love—qualities that not only enrich our personal journey but also strengthen the fabric of our communities.

Our world often glorifies the "go-getter"—the individual who relentlessly pursues success, power, and prestige. Yet, this frantic chase is a mirage that leads to emptiness and deterioration. The person who spends their life chasing after material toys or fleeting fame is assured of one outcome: bad health, both physically and spiritually. Ulcers eat away at their stomach; strained muscles give way; taut nerves unravel. Such a person sets out to beat the universe, but no one can subdue the cosmic order established by God.

The ego-driven life focuses on personal glory rather than God's glory. It seeks recognition and validation from the world instead of finding fulfillment in serving God's Kingdom. This path can lead to exhaustion, dissatisfaction, and a sense of emptiness, as it lacks the sustaining power of divine purpose.

The "go-getter" operates in vain, lacking the humility to recognize that all things are orchestrated by a mighty Lord who inhabits all places and times. Without this understanding, they become like a molecule vibrating and rebounding erratically within the limits they've imposed upon themselves. They lack a design to their life because they fail to see the dynamic design of life itself—a design rooted in divine purpose and order.

It's important to recognize that the material world is not inherently evil or to be shunned. God created the physical universe and declared it good. The key is to engage with the material world through the lens of spiritual understanding. Wealth, success, and possessions are not problematic in themselves; it is our attachment to them and the motivations behind our pursuit of them that can lead us astray.

But let's be clear: nobody achieves anything by "going out and getting it" in the worldly sense. That very premise insinuates that whatever one is after belongs to somebody else and must be taken away. When a person has created, on the plane of the mind, the conviction that whatever they are after is already theirs, they will be guided along the proper paths and into the proper actions that will manifest their Mined Matter.

We often define ourselves by external labels: our job titles, positions, neighborhoods, affiliations, or even zodiac signs. However, these are mere descriptors of who we seem to be, not who we truly are. They are vain titles of nobility that can distract us from our authentic selves.

God reminds us to place no limits on our thinking and to recognize our limitless potential through Christ:

"And I will give unto thee the keys of the kingdom of heaven: and whatsoever thou shalt bind on earth shall be bound in heaven: and whatsoever thou shalt loose on earth shall be loosed in heaven."
(Matthew 16:19 KJV)

"I can do all things through Christ which strengtheneth me."
(Philippians 4:13 KJV)

You may run into setbacks, into circumstances that appear to be preventing you from arriving at your destination, but these are not setbacks at all; they are steps forward. In fact, they are the only steps forward possible for you to make and still arrive at your goal. Since you don't know everything or can call on the vast resources of the Subconscious Mind, you cannot predict the path by which it will take you to your destination; even if that path is directly through a Federal Prison.

In your own limited knowledge of the things and circumstances and motives of the world, you may decide that in order to arrive at your destination it is necessary for you to take a certain step at a certain time at a certain place, when the truth is that such a step actually taken would result in disaster. When you are frustrated in taking this altered step, you visualize the defeat of your plans and come to believe that evil has been visited on you instead of good. Just like when Peter looked around at the circumstances by looking away from Jesus and sank. Thus, you lose your trust in God and the immutable Dynamic Laws of the universe.

There is absolutely only one way to make the law work in your favor, and that is to trust it completely and not try to predict it or evaluate the circumstances. The moment you start predicting the path or evaluating the circumstances you should take toward any goal, you will find your NOW faith challenged at every fork in the road, at every by-path, at every apparent obstacle. But when you have learned to trust the Laws and Dynamics of Life completely, you will begin to see every delay and every obstacle as opportunities whereby you may become fit and ready for what awaits you when you arrive at your destination. *"My brethren, count it all joy when ye fall into divers temptations; Knowing this, that the trying of your faith worketh patience. But let patience have her perfect work, that ye may be perfect and entire, wanting nothing."* (James 1:2-4 KJV)

There is no such thing as failure unless it is accepted. There is no such thing as defeat unless it is accepted. Only what you accept comes to you finally, all else is but temporary and merely a step to your goal. Such is the Dynamic Law of Attraction, a law that never fails.

In moments of solitude—whether in a quiet room, atop a hillside, or overlooking the vast ocean—you are invited to turn your thoughts inward. Slow your breathing until you feel complete peace and relaxation. Retreat into the depths of your being until your thoughts become streams flowing through your mind. Then ask yourself, "Who is this that observes?"

This introspection reveals the real you—a mighty truth and a clarion call in this great age. Let the spiritual man rule your life. Surrender your challenges to Christ and listen attentively for His guidance. When the answers come, accept them with complete confidence and NOW faith.

Our minds are battlegrounds where thoughts shape our reality. Vain imaginations can stealthily infiltrate like thieves in the night, robbing us of our greatest treasures—peace, joy, purpose. We must close our minds to all lack, limitation, and disease. Instead, we should fill our consciousness with thoughts that operate perfectly in accordance with the Laws and Dynamics of Life established by God.

By directing our thoughts intentionally, we align ourselves with divine principles and open the door to transformative blessings.

A fundamental truth governs our existence: All things must be paid for; mutual exchange is a Dynamic Law. You receive because you first give. There is no such thing as true independence; we are all interdependent parts of a greater whole.

Jesus illustrates this principle:

"Give, and it shall be given unto you; good measure, pressed down, and shaken together, and running over, shall men give into your bosom. For with the same measure that ye mete withal it shall be measured to you again." (Luke 6:38 KJV)

We cannot live without our neighbors, and they cannot live without us. What we contribute to others, they return to us in kind. This exchange may come in various forms—money, time, support, kindness—but the law remains steadfast: the exchange is always equal, regardless of how it may appear in the moment.

King David understood the importance of integrity and mutual exchange. When offered a gift that cost him nothing, he insisted on paying the full price:

"But the king replied to Araunah, 'No, I insist on paying you for it. I will not sacrifice to the Lord my God burnt offerings that cost me nothing.' So David bought the threshing floor and the oxen and paid fifty shekels of silver for them." (2 Samuel 24:24 NIV)

David's refusal to offer a sacrifice that cost him nothing underscores the value of integrity and honor in our dealings. It reinforces that there are no bargains when it comes to divine principles; we must invest authentically to reap genuine rewards.

Integrity is more than honesty; it's the alignment of our actions with divine truth, even when no one is watching. It's about being true to our word, honoring our commitments, and conducting ourselves with moral uprightness. Just as David's story in the bible demonstrates the observance of the Law of Mutual Exchange, another story in Acts tells of the ultimate price of transgression of this law:

"Now a man named Ananias, together with his wife Sapphira, also sold a piece of property. With his wife's full knowledge he kept back part of the money for himself, but brought the rest and put it at the apostles' feet. Then Peter said, "Ananias, how is it that Satan has so filled your heart that you have lied to the Holy Spirit and have kept for yourself some of the money you received for the land? Didn't it belong to you before it was sold? And after it was sold, wasn't the money at your disposal? What made you think of doing such a thing? You have not lied just to human beings but to God." When Ananias heard this, he fell down and died. And great fear seized all who heard what had happened. Then some young men came forward, wrapped up his body, and carried him out and buried him. About three hours later his wife came in, not knowing what had happened. Peter asked her, "Tell me, is this the price you and Ananias got for the land?" "Yes," she said, "that is the price." Peter said to her, "How could you conspire to test the Spirit of the Lord? Listen! The feet of the men who buried your husband are at the door, and they will carry you out also." At that moment she fell down at his feet and died. Then the young men came in and, finding her dead, carried her out and buried her beside her husband. Great fear seized the whole church and all who heard about these events." (Acts 5:1-11 NIV)

The book of Proverbs teaches:

"A false balance and dishonest business practices are extremely offensive to the Lord, but an accurate scale is His delight." (Proverbs 11:1 AMP)

In our personal and professional lives, we must uphold fairness and justice. Whether in business transactions, relationships, or everyday interactions, integrity should be the hallmark of our conduct. This commitment builds trust, fosters healthy relationships, and aligns us with God's favor.

Honor also involves recognizing and respecting the inherent value and authority of others. By honoring authorities—whether in government, the workplace, or the home—we demonstrate humility and respect for divine order. Moreover, Paul instructs us:

"Give to everyone what you owe them: If you owe taxes, pay taxes; if revenue, then revenue; if respect, then respect; if honor, then honor."
(Romans 13:7 NIV)

Honor extends beyond authority figures; it encompasses everyone we interact with. By showing respect and valuing others, we foster an environment of mutual appreciation and cooperation. At the core of mutual exchange is love—the highest commandment and the essence of God's character. Paul encapsulates this beautifully:

"Let no debt remain outstanding, except the continuing debt to love one another, for whoever loves others has fulfilled the law."
(Romans 13:8 NIV)

Love is an ongoing commitment that never reaches a point of completion. It's a perpetual debt we joyfully pay, knowing that it enriches both giver and receiver. This love is selfless, sacrificial, and unconditional—a reflection of God's love for us. By loving our neighbors as ourselves, we honor God's greatest commandments and participate in the divine nature. Jesus affirmed:

"A new command I give you: Love one another. As I have loved you, so you must love one another." (John 13:34 NIV)

To live in integrity, honor, and love, we must daily reject vanity and selfish ambition. Disdain the pursuit of empty titles and the relentless striving of the "go-getter." Instead, move with dignity, surety, and purpose, guided by the wisdom and direction of the Mind of Christ.

Do not obsess over actions or outcomes. Recognize that thought produces action as naturally as light emanates from the sun. All decisions are birthed in the Conscious and carried out by the Subconscious Mind that is connected with the Mind of Christ. Therefore, think positively; refuse to accept negative circumstances as definitive. Keep your thoughts steadfast on what is good, and fuel your vision with NOW faith.

When we align our thoughts with the Mind of Christ, we step into a realm of limitless possibilities—where the universe opens itself to us, overflowing with abundance, power, and love. In this space, we discover that life is not meant to be driven by vanity or the fleeting pursuit of status, but rather by purpose, integrity, and the selfless love that God has woven into His divine design. By tuning our minds to His frequency, we unlock the boundless rewards of living in harmony with His eternal laws, walking in adventure, power, and a deep sense of fulfillment.

One of the first steps toward living in this divine flow is cultivating integrity. This means being honest in all that we do—letting our "yes" be yes and our "no" be no. We uphold our commitments, not because it's easy or convenient, but because our word is a reflection of the character God has placed within us. Integrity goes hand in hand with honoring others. Showing respect for authority and valuing those we encounter daily isn't just a social courtesy; it's a divine command. Through empathy, consideration, and humility, we elevate those around us, creating a ripple effect of honor and respect that transforms relationships and communities.

Finally, the greatest of all these principles is love. When we make love a priority, we reflect the very heart of God. Love isn't simply a feeling—it's an action, a decision to serve, uplift, and care for others even when it costs us. As we align our thoughts with truth, guarding our minds from negativity and embracing the promises of God, we release the need for vanity-driven pursuits. By trusting in divine order, we relinquish the compulsion to control every outcome, knowing that God's plan is always for our good. Living in integrity, honor, and love is not just a principle—it is a lifestyle that aligns us with the very heartbeat of heaven, making us conduits of His grace and blessings to the world around us.

Remember, whatsoever you think will manifest in your life. Choose thoughts that reflect integrity, honor, and love. As you do, you'll discover a life enriched with purpose, joy, and the immeasurable rewards that come from living in harmony with divine principles.

Heavenly Father, we thank You for the timeless principles of integrity, honor, and love. Help us to embody these qualities in every aspect of our lives. Guide our thoughts, words, and actions so that they align with Your perfect will. May we live out the Law of Mutual Exchange, becoming vessels of Your grace and instruments of Your peace. In Jesus' name, we pray. Amen.

| 10 |

Unshakable NOW Faith-Power of Present-Tense Belief

*E*mbrace the dynamic force of NOW faith to unlock God's promises and live in present victory, transforming your life one demonstration at a time.

In the journey of life, there exists a powerful force that can propel us beyond our limitations and into the realm of limitless possibilities. This force is **NOW faith**—a present, immediate, and unshakable trust in God's promises and timing. Living in the present with NOW faith is not merely about hopeful anticipation; it's about actively embracing the reality of God's provision here and now. When we master this art, we unlock transformative power that reshapes our personal and spiritual lives.

The power of NOW faith is anchored in the scriptural declaration:

"Now faith is the substance of things hoped for, the evidence of things not seen." (Hebrews 11:1 KJV)

This faith is not passive; it is a dynamic, present-tense confidence in God's Word and His immutable laws. It transcends mere belief and becomes a living force that shapes our reality. NOW faith is the activation of our trust in God's promises, fully expecting them to manifest in our lives. Central to understanding NOW faith is grasping the Law of Sowing and Reaping—an unbreakable divine command integral to the dynamic law of creation. *"Do not be deceived: God cannot be mocked. A man reaps what he sows."* (Galatians 6:7 NIV)

When we sow seeds of faith, obedience, and thankfulness, we position ourselves to reap the harvest of God's promises. Conversely, sowing seeds of arrogance, greed, or impatience sets us against the flow of God's will, leading to frustration and disappointment.

Consider the desire for a material item that has one so obsessed on it that they are willing to sacrifice anyone or anything to get it, such as a luxury car. Wanting a brand new Bentley is not inherently wrong. However, if that desire stems from envy or lust, it creates undue pressure, causes one's finances to be strained, and may not align with God's timing or will for your life. Proverbs warns us:

"Since, then, you have been raised with Christ, set your hearts on things above, where Christ is, seated at the right hand of God. Set your minds on things above, not on earthly things." (Colossians 3:1-2 NIV)

When we attempt to force our will, we risk tearing down what God is building. Without sowing the right seeds—preparation, patience, and trust—there can be no authentic harvest. The ultimate lesson in living with NOW Faith is learning to let go of your own will. Not passive but an active trust in God's plan and timing.

"Now listen, you who say, 'Today or tomorrow we will go to this or that city, spend a year there, carry on business and make money.' Why, you do not even know what will happen tomorrow... Instead, you ought to say, 'If it is the Lord's will, we will live and do this or that.'" (James 4:13-15 NIV)

Approach your goals and desires with a heart of acceptance: "If it is the Lord's will, I will receive this." This attitude reflects the childlike faith Jesus commends—trusting that God knows best and will provide what is truly needed, when it is truly needed. When we relinquish control and align ourselves with God's will, we open the door for Him to bless us beyond our imagination.

"Now to Him who is able to do immeasurably more than all we ask or imagine, according to His power that is at work within us."
(Ephesians 3:20 NIV)

It's not our will that brings creation into being but God's power and grace that make all things possible. Many strive to manifest their desires through sheer determination, believing that willpower alone can shape reality. However, this approach often leads to frustration. James cautions us against this mindset:

"Why, you do not even know what will happen tomorrow... All such boasting is evil." (James 4:14,16 NIV)

Declaring "I will make money" or "I will achieve success" without acknowledging God's sovereignty is walking in arrogance. True dynamic law doesn't respond to force or human determination but to belief and attunement to God's will. We cannot MAKE anything happen outside His divine laws. Instead, we must sow seeds in the spirit and trust God to bring forth the image, then the harvest.

Replace demanding and forcing outcomes with expectation and acceptance. Jesus taught that faith as small as a mustard seed can move mountains (Matthew 17:20). He emphasized the importance of childlike faith—a trust that doesn't force but confidently expects. It's not about demanding wealth or success; it's about accepting the abundance already present in God's creation and knowing He provides according to His will.

"And my God will meet all your needs according to the riches of His glory in Christ Jesus." (Philippians 4:19 NIV)

Notice, it says "needs"—not always our wants, and certainly not outside God's timing or plan for our lives. The Subconscious Mind is designed to nurture and cause things to grow in accordance to God's riches and glory. Just as the earth allows any seed to flourish, the Subconscious Mind transforms the seeds of thought—planted through the Conscious Mind by the Mind of Christ—into image downloads and ultimately physical reality. Once a seed is planted, it will inevitably grow and manifest unless choked out, uprooted, and/or replaced. As we discuss sowing and reaping, I am reminded of my lesson in seed time & harvest time gardening at a young age.

I have but very few events from early childhood that I remember, they range from the very vivid to the cloudy at best. One of such vivid memories is of a gardening lesson from Ms. Rosie Jackson. Ms. Rosie was an avid gardener, and she shared many stories with me of her beautiful and large garden back at her old house. You see Ms. Rosie had recently moved into the neighborhood next door to our house at on South Matthisen Avenue, in Compton, California. I was six-years old and just started the 1st grade at Dickerson Elementary School. I was a "talkative" lad and Ms. Rosie was a perfect recruit to share my many tells to, like how I was an honorary team member of the G.I. Joes and could do all the rescue moves. I was more than happy to drive over with my "Joe Van", and I even let Ms. Rosie work the lever to activate G.I. Joe's "Kung-Fu Grip". She really seemed to enjoy G.I. Joe as much as I did, or at least to a six-year-old boy, it did.

Every morning before I went off to school, I would climb over my fence and would always find Ms. Rosie sitting in her "fishing chair", as she called it, looking at the grass by the back fence. She would always be in the perfect position for me to share my many adventures of the school yard, like the story about the new kid who always looked at me "mean". I would tell these stories to Ms. Rosie for as long as I could until I heard the call from my mom telling me it's time to go to school. I would always tell Ms. Rosie that I would finish my story when I got home. She would always smile and say she couldn't wait to hear it.

Well, this particular story about the "mean" new kid had a final climax and I couldn't wait to tell Ms. Rosie I took her advice, and it had a surprising ending. You see, what I didn't know as a six-year-old is the "mean" looking kid had a unibrow and whether laughing or frowning, he looked mean. So, every day for about a week (it felt like the whole school year), this kid would walk over towards me, look at me and move his head in such a way as to say, "I'm coming for you!" This ritual happened at the beginning of recess as well as the lunch break. As he got close, I would take of running and he would oblige me by chasing me. From the time I made eye contact with him until the class bell rang, I was running for my life, and he was chasing behind. I guess the good news is that I was faster and even though a few close calls, he never caught me.

Well on that morning before school as I told Ms. Rosie about me running all over the school (can you imagine a G.I. Joe running all day!), her advice for me was to stop running and ask him why he was chasing me. So, when I got home that day to find Ms. Rosie in her "fishing chair", told her I did exactly what she told me to do and to both of our surprises, his answer was, "because you ran, I ran with you, I thought we were playing!" Imagine that, so I'm happy to report that the "unibrow" became one of my best friends as he pretended to be a villain to the Joe's. Crisis over.

Now I often wondered why Ms. Rosie was always sitting in the same place each day but never asked her. Since I learned from her to ask the question, when you are not sure, I asked what she was doing. She told me that she used to live at her home with her mom and used to care for her beautiful garden she planted with her own hands every day. It had all sorts of vegetables and fruits that she would cook such wonderful meals that fed her family from it. She would also "can" fruit as well as save some in Mason Jars to eat later or give to family.

She really missed her garden and ever since her and her mom moved in with her daughter, she just continued to do what she did every day and that's tending her garden. She asked me, "do you see it?" I told Ms. Rosie, that I'm' six-years old now, and not so easily fooled as when I was five, and I said to her, "no, all I see is grass". She said, "not with your eyes, but with your imagination, as she began to point and show me every row the fruits and vegetables were planted. She was so vivid in her description that I "could" begin to see the garden. I said," Ms. Rosie, you forgot the strawberries, I love strawberries. She said, "well, you just planted them over there on the edge where you can pick them whenever you want to eat some". "I can see them", I said. "This is fun, when are we going to plant "our" garden?" She said, "well now that you can see it, we can start"

Ms. Rosie was 65-years old, and her mother was 82, both full of life and both had full mastery of their mental faculties. Grandma Ardie, everyone called her was Ms. Rosie's mom, and she would sometimes come out to see the garden too. You see, it was no coincidence that Ms. Rosie and Grandma Ardie lived next door to me, you see Ms. Rosie's daughter that moved her in with her was my grandmother, Hazel. Sara, her daughter and my mom, never lived too far from her and is why we lived next door. My grandmother, Hazel, always wanted to have her whole family close by, she used to say she wanted all the generations to always be together. As much as she tried in her own efforts, most of our family just wanted their own space. But not my mom and not me! I guess that is where I get such a strong desire for family gatherings. Ms. Rosie was my great-grandmother, we all called Mama, and Grandma Ardie was my great-great grandmother and I'm' happy to say, even though very young, I had the privilege to know and talk to them both and enjoy their wisdom.

One Saturday morning I peeked over the fence to see my uncles tearing up the grass in the area where our garden was to be planted. By the end of the day all that was left of that section of the back yard was a perfect rectangle of dirt. The next morning, I found Mama back in her "fishing chair" still looking at the new garden. When she saw me, she said, "The dirt is almost ready". What I now know is that Mama was super charging her ability to see the garden in her faculty of imagination.

Imagination in your thoughts mixed with powerful positive emotions will drive those thoughts into your Subconscious Mind, as they did in mine. Once those thoughts of vivid imagination dominate your Conscious Mind it is transferred to the where the Subconscious Mind seeks out the material (Matter) manifestation by the most practical media available to it. Two of the transmitting agents are the Law of Confession combined with the principle of positive affirmations. Every time Mama infused her imagination into my thoughts, a vivid picture exploded in my mind until I too could "see" the finished garden, especially my strawberries. I could taste them. Whatever you hold in your Subconscious Mind and "feel" with regular affirmative thoughts, feed it with daily confessions, you affect a transfer of though impulse from your spirit to your Subconscious Mind, it will hand you over the Matter manifestation of the thoughts dominating in a man. *"As a man thinketh in his heart, so is he".*

This supercharged imagination fills the heart with belief and out of the abundance of the heart, the mouth speaks. Giving voice to the thought impulses of imagination now fuels your faith. This is the basis for Now faith. "Faith comes by hearing" and hearing and hearing... To build faith, like a muscle under tension, you must use yours as well as other words in agreement with your confession and that causes your NOW faith to grow. You must stay in the, voluntary, mindset of NOW faith for as long as it takes the material manifestation. Once that manifestation occurs, it's time to increase your demand on NOW faith and repeat the process until you shorten the "waiting" time. Your goal should be to increase your demand on FAITH and repeat the process by working your NOW faith muscle until you shorten the "waiting" time. Your goal is - "NOW FAITH IS". You put a demand, and it shows up in material manifestation, immediately as the Mind of Christ has demonstrated. "Be ye imitators of God as dear children" (Ephesians 5:1 AMP)

As God has caused me to look back and remember he wonderful lessons of my 65-year-old great grandma I now see that He kept her alive long enough to imbed in me, through physical demonstration, the most important examples of: "NOW faith"; "*death and life are in power of the tongue, and those that love it shall eat the fruit thereof*"; "*Be not deceived; God is not mocked: for whatsoever a man soweth, that shall he also reap*" (Galatians 6:7); "*Any weed that I did not plant I shall root out*"; and most importantly the whole parable of the Sower. This lesson by Mama demonstrated the patience to work the dirt and wait until all weeds could have no effect on the crops before planting occurred. The biggest revelation of the parable of the Sower is the meaning of the parable's ending lines.

"*But others fell into good ground, and brought forth fruit, some an hundredfold, some sixtyfold, some thirtyfold.*" (Matthew 13:8 KJV).

When I asked Mama why she was still staring at our garden and why we we're not plating our strawberries, she told me "The dirt is not ready". "Mama, it looks ready to me, see I can see the strawberries right over here on the end", I replied. "Yes son, I can see them, but I also see that if we plant your strawberries in the field today, the leftover roots of the weeds you can't see right now will kill most of the strawberries", she said. Then she pointed at the freshly watered garden dirt and said, "Don't you see those leftover weeds over here and over there? Well, they must be pulled out before you plant your strawberries, because those weeds have been in that ground a long time and the weed thinks they own our garden." "These are the stubborn weeds that did not come out with your uncle's picking, raking and hoeing; these have to be plucked out by the root by hand as they show up to get some water", Mama instructed. At that moment I saw just how many stubborn weeds were still in our garden and remember thinking, this is going to be hard.

This is why the enemy likes being in church, he will drink the water of worship as well just to see who among them he might devour. We must be vigilant in the weeding process and not be lazy or in such a rush that we compromise our desired hundredfold crop down to a mere thirtyfold because we refused to do the necessary dirt work first. To my male readers, you don't want a thirtyfold harvest in your crops, and you don't want a thirtyfold wife. You want an hundredfold wife, now do the necessary dirt work!

After a week of waiting at night and pulling by day, I stood beside Mama looking over our garden and I remember her look of complete satisfaction as she said, "Now it's ready for your strawberries, son". Not only that but looking at the perfectly straight rows of mounds of dirt, she pointed at each row and named each vegetable and fruit she already saw. She said, "Over there is my "maetas" (tomatoes), over there is my "taetas" (potatoes), and there are my mustards, my collards, my turnips, my onions, corn, cabbage, lettuce, peas, black-eyed peas, green beans, Limas, watermelon, grapes, honeydews", and so on until she finally got to the good part. And over there is you're your strawberries, she said smiling and winking at me. Then she took me to the back of the garden, along the back fence and said, "Back here is going to be your favorite, it was mine when I was a little girl. Over here will be the sugar cane."

"I don't think I could be happier at the toy store buying new GI Joe accessories than when I saw Mama going row by row picking out our garden seeds. Even my grandmother looked happy, I think she could taste the garden grub because she was used to it. It was time to plant; finally, our garden would be underway! Surprisingly, the next morning before school, I found Mama still patrolling for stubborn weeds and not yet planting the seeds. In my excitement, I asked her if she was waiting for me. She said, yes, be here early Saturday morning, that's when we plant, I am just making sure no more weeds grow until then.

Of course, as you might imagine it was a lovely garden our family ate out of it for many years even after Mama went on home to be with the Lord. My strawberries were sweet and delicious, and everyone would ask me if they could have some, there was so many I couldn't say no. The "yellow meat" watermelon, the brightest and sweetest you ever tasted. Me and my cousins enjoyed many summers in that back yard having watermelon seed spitting contests. But Mama was right, every time I pulled out my pocketknife, shucked that sugar cane and chewed the pure joy of sweetness that tasted better than candy, I thought of my great grandma as a little girl. Mama left me with something much better than a garden or strawberries; she demonstrated great NOW faith with an absolute expectancy that this grass would one day be a garden that would feed us for years. And before we finally left those two homes in Compton, all our family took great pride in keeping Mama alive and sharing her love by tending "her" garden year after year, especially me. Guarding that dirt against weed roots is the exact process we must do to the strongholds of the mind in the realm of thought. Every thought you entertain and accept becomes a part of you and inevitably brings forth the physical reality of your image. All choice is made in the Conscious Mind, and all acceptance occurs through the Subconscious Mind, facilitated by a spirit-to-Spirit transfer. By understanding that the Mind of Christ works in harmony with our Subconscious Mind, we recognize the importance of the thoughts we choose to accept. There are two frequencies at play:

1. Sensory Input Frequency: Processes the physical world through our five senses, dealing with doubt and fear.
2. Attunement-Based Discernment Frequency: Engages matters of the spirit through prayer, praise, worship, love and faith.

When we attune ourselves to the latter frequency, we align with the Mind of Christ, enabling the manifestation of our accepted thoughts through NOW faith and conviction. Understanding the dynamics of the mind reveals that the differences between individuals are often just illusions. One may have experienced lack or limitation, but when we cast down these imaginations and renew our thinking to embrace abundance and health, we change our "I"—our self-concept—and become a new person. *"Do not conform to the pattern of this world, but be transformed by the renewing of your mind."* (Romans 12:2 NIV) Your surroundings will change, and your body will become vigorous and purposeful, animated by the greatest power in the universe. You can be anything you want to be, do anything you want to do. Your background makes no difference.

Exposed to the childhood adversity and trauma, you can use as steppingstones to the stars, for the Kingdom of God is within you, and all the power of the mighty Mind of Christ awaits your choice, belief, and acceptance in NOW faith.

"I can do all things through Christ who strengthens me."
(Philippians 4:13 NKJV)

No one, regardless of their social status or the circumstances they are born into, is granted more human potential than another. Whether cradled in wealth or raised in humility, we all stand equal before the Everlasting Father, each possessing the same infinite possibilities. Contrary to popular belief, vanity—rooted in the false perception of separation from the Mind of Christ—often festers more among those facing hardship, failure, and suffering than among those who have achieved success or live in health. For vanity, in its essence, is nothing more than the inflated sense of self-reliance, detached from the divine purpose and responsibility placed within each of us.

It's vanity and isolated ego that become our undoing. Phrases like "I have to do this" or "I will make this happen" reflect a misplaced sense of personal responsibility, separating us from God's power. The truth is, the "I" does nothing but choose and accept the images as answers to our prayers; all manifestations are done by God through the Mind of Christ. Understanding this liberates us from undue stress and aligns us with divine purpose.

The ultimate use of our will is not to force outcomes but to choose our thoughts. By willfully choosing thoughts that align with God's Word and promises, we set in motion the dynamic laws that bring those thoughts into reality and master the art of maintaining our NOW faith.

"For as he thinks in his heart, so is he." (Proverbs 23:7 NKJV)

Once you've defined the Matter of your desired situation and your general objectives in your Conscious Mind, let go. Release the problem and trust God to provide the solution. One day, while engaged in daily activities, the answer will emerge, striking your consciousness with clarity and removing all doubt. This is the Wonderful Counselor communicating with your spirit on a frequency beyond conscious reasoning reaping your NOW faith with the rewards of your desired answer.

This guidance isn't achieved through effort or will but through confidence and NOW faith in the laws and dynamics of life, which are greater than our own understanding. It comes from complete acceptance of the Mighty God and Prince of Peace as the power working within us.

When you trust God's laws wholly, delays and obstacles become opportunities for growth, preparing you for what awaits at your destination. You begin to see that every delay works in your favor and may even begin to see this as divine assignments and appointments as you connect with the people and circumstances in your daily walk towards your desires.

The art of maintaining your NOW faith is patience. Patience is not idle waiting but active trust in God's perfect timing. It's a dynamic state of confidence in God's sovereignty, where we consciously choose to submit our agendas to Him, believing that His plans surpass our own. When God delays, it's not a sign of neglect or indifference; rather, it's an invitation to deepen our trust in Him. We must rely on God to accomplish His will through us by His power, not by our own efforts. This trust shifts our focus from our circumstances to God's unchanging nature.

The Bible reveals that God's delays serve purposeful roles in our lives, often beyond our immediate understanding. Here are several reasons why God might delay and how they contribute to our growth:

1. Protection:

God may delay protecting you from unseen harm. Just as a parent might hold back a child from running into danger, God, in His omniscience, knows what lies ahead and intervenes accordingly. He desires to further His work in and through you, ensuring that you are kept safe from situations that could derail His plans.

Consider how a closed door or missed opportunity sometimes leads to something better down the line. What initially feels like a setback may actually be God shielding you from harm or positioning you for greater blessings.

1. Faith Growth:

Delays can be a fertile ground for growing your faith. When answers aren't immediate, you learn to lean not on your understanding but on God's faithfulness. This period of waiting refines your character, teaching you perseverance and deepening your relationship with Him.

"Consider it pure joy, my brothers and sisters, whenever you face trials of many kinds, because you know that the testing of your faith produces perseverance." (James 1:2-3 NIV)

1. Greater Purpose:

God's delays often align with a greater purpose that transcends our personal desires. He orchestrates events in a way that not only benefits us but also fulfills His overarching plan. Our waiting becomes a crucial piece in a much larger puzzle.

Joseph's journey from slavery to becoming a ruler in Egypt involved significant delays and hardships. Yet, those delays positioned him to save many lives during a famine (Genesis 50:20).

1. God's Timing:

God's timing is perfect, even when it doesn't align with our schedules. He sees the end from the beginning and knows the optimal moment to act. Delays may occur because the answer we seek isn't fitting within His divine timetable yet. Our job is to understand that, "every delay works in our favor".

"He has made everything beautiful in its time." (Ecclesiastes 3:11 NIV)

1. Relying on God:

Sometimes, God delays to teach us reliance on Him. Our success isn't solely the product of our efforts but a result of His grace working through us. By delaying, God reminds us that we need to depend on His strength rather than our own. In moments of delay, shifting your reliance from self to God can lead to spiritual breakthroughs and a deeper sense of peace.

1. Understanding God's Season:

God's time is when He knows you're ready, not necessarily when you think you are. He prepares you for what's ahead, ensuring that when the blessing comes, you're equipped to handle it responsibly. Your job in this is to accept this as truth and believe.

Just as a gardener waits for the right season to plant seeds to ensure optimal growth, God waits for the right season in your life to bring certain things to fruition.

1. Doing Your Part:

While God is faithful to do His part, we must not delay in doing ours. Active patience involves deep listening, obedience, preparation, and engagement in the tasks God has placed before us. It's about being diligent in the present while trusting Him with the future.

1. Avoiding Distance from God:

Distancing yourself from God can inadvertently delay His blessings. Staying close to Him through prayer, worship, and reading His

Word keeps your heart aligned with His, making you more receptive to His guidance and timing.

When you neglect your relationship with God, you open the door to unnecessary delays in the fulfillment of His plans for your life. It is essential to prioritize your spiritual walk, keeping your steps aligned with His divine direction. Neglect doesn't always come in obvious forms; often, it presents itself through subtle distractions—like endlessly scrolling through Facebook, TikTok, YouTube, or other social media platforms, unaware of the time slipping away. These distractions creep in quietly, and when brought to your attention, you may find yourself becoming defensive, justifying your choices as harmless or even beneficial. But beware—these seemingly innocent diversions can gradually pull you away from your true purpose, dulling your awareness of God's voice and delaying the manifestation of His promises.

Reflecting on delayed answered prayer, it's evident that patience is an active engagement with God's process. Yogi Berra famously said about baseball games, "It ain't over till it's over." The same principle applies to our spiritual journey, or sanctification. It's an ongoing process that continues until we meet the Lord. Even if we've yielded our lives to Jesus, there's always more to surrender. God's delays often reveal areas where we need to yield further to Him, exposing parts of our character that require refinement.

Consider the anecdote of Mrs. Einstein. When asked if she understood her husband's theory of relativity, she replied, "No, but I know Albert, and he can be trusted." Similarly, as Christians, we might not grasp why God makes us wait, especially when we desire immediate answers. But we know God's character—He is loving, faithful, and just. Our understanding is limited, but His wisdom is infinite.

In the journey of life, there will be moments when circumstances seem unclear, but it is in those very moments that we must anchor ourselves in the unshakable truth of God's character. Trust, not understanding, is what allows us to reap the full rewards of His promises. Surrendering our personal agendas to Him is an act of NOW faith that acknowledges His infinite wisdom, for His ways are far higher than our own (Isaiah 55:8-9). The process we often resist is actually the very means by which He prepares us for what lies ahead—waiting is never wasted in the Kingdom of God. Instead, it is a divine season of growth, refinement, and alignment with His perfect will. In the meantime, we are called to stay faithful in obedience and service, knowing that every step of faithfulness is seen by God and honored in due time. Trusting Him fully, even when the path is unclear, positions us to receive far more than we could ever plan or imagine.

Patience is about actively trusting God's perfect timing and His sovereign plan for our lives. It's a deliberate choice to rest in His promises, confident that He is working all things together for our good (Romans 8:28). By embracing patience, we allow God to shape us, protect us, and ultimately lead us into the fullness of His blessings. Remember, delays are not denials or failures; they are often divine interventions designed for our benefit and His glory.

Remember, failure is permanent only if you chose to accept it. Defeat is not an external event but an internal decision. Only what you accept becomes final; all else is temporary as you move toward your goal.

Don't constantly examine your goals to see if you've attained them. Fixating on the outcome projects anxiety into your Subconscious Mind, and projecting instead with greater conviction the thing you fear most, hindering your accepted image for manifestation. Instead, focus on maintaining NOW faith, trusting that God's timing is perfect.

To truly live in the present and embrace the transformative power of NOW faith, you must first guard your thoughts diligently. Every thought is a seed that either produces fruit or weeds in the garden of your life. By choosing thoughts that align with God's promises and rejecting doubt and negativity, you sow seeds of NOW faith, obedience, and thankfulness. The harvest you reap tomorrow is directly tied to the seeds you plant today. Your life today is an exact production of the seeds you've sown into your heart in the yesterdays of your life. Your future focus must be on sowing good seeds, knowing that what you put into the ground with conviction will be brought to fruition in its due season.

However, while sowing is vital, equally important is releasing control over the outcome. Too often, we try to force results, but NOW faith demands that we trust in God's sovereignty and perfect timing. Letting go of the need to manipulate or rush the process allows God's divine order to unfold in ways that far exceed our limited understanding. As you maintain a positive expectation, rooted in the assurance that God is working all things for your benefit, you begin to walk with an unwavering confidence, anticipating His goodness in every situation.

Living in the power of NOW faith means staying attuned to the guidance of the Holy Spirit, cultivating a deep connection through prayer, meditation, and quiet listening. This spiritual sensitivity ensures that you take steps only as led by God, not by your own understanding or fear. Acting in NOW faith is not about striving in your strength but about surrendering to God's guidance, knowing that He is directing your path. By integrating this NOW faith into every aspect of your life, you shift from anxiety to peace, from limitation to abundance, unlocking the full potential of God's promises for your life.

> *"Therefore I say to you, whatever things you ask when you pray, believe that you receive them, and you will have them."* (Mark 11:24 NKJV)

If you sow the seeds of faith, obedience, and thankfulness, you will reap the harvest of God's promises. On the contrary, if you sow in arrogance, greed, or demanding, you will face opposition rather than cooperation with God's will. When we attempt to force our will, we often end up tearing down what God is trying to build.

The ultimate lesson in living in the present and reaping the rewards, is learning to let go of your will as an active trust in God's plan and His timing. When you pray or meditate, approach it with the heart of acceptance: *"If it is the Lord's will, I will receive this."* This attitude reflects the childlike NOW faith that Jesus called us to have, trusting that God knows best and will always provide what is truly needed.

When we finally let go of our own desires and align ourselves with God's will, we open the door for Him to bless us far beyond what we could imagine. Ephesians 3:20 assures us: *"Now to him who is able to do immeasurably more than all we ask or imagine, according to his power that is at work within us."*

The power of the word must be coupled with NOW faith, acceptance, and submission to God's will. When we trust that God's dynamic laws will bring forth the harvest in His perfect time, we experience the abundance and peace that surpass all understanding. Remember, it is not your will that brings creation into being, but God's power and grace that make all things possible.

Also, we must remember that the Subconscious Mind is the fertile garden of the heart, designed solely to nurture and cause Matter to grow. Just as the earth allows any seed to flourish, the Subconscious Mind transforms both the seeds of thought—Mined and planted by the Conscious Mind—into the physical reality of Matter. The seed, once planted and undisturbed, will inevitably grow and manifest itself in the physical world.

Many people, in their pursuit of transforming their spiritual and personal lives, attempt to force their desires into reality, thinking that determination alone is enough to manifest their wants. James 4:13-16 warns us against this mindset which speaks to the futility of imposing our will on life without first seeking God's will.

As believers, we must replace demanding and forcing outcomes with expectation and acceptance. Jesus taught that faith as small as a mustard seed can move mountains, but He also emphasized the importance of childlike NOW faith. A child doesn't force anything to happen—they simply trust that their needs will be met. In the same way, we must trust in God's dynamic laws of creation, attraction, and abundance.

Using the frequency of the Subconscious Mind, the Mind of Christ begins the process of manifesting those accepted thoughts back to the yielded spirit in NOW faith and conviction. When you truly have come to understand that there are two frequencies; one for (AM) processing with the five senses the Sarx world around it, as well as dealing with doubt & fear and one for (FM) processing God's images and manifestations of the spirit through prayer, love & NOW faith.

Embracing NOW faith is a transformative practice that invites us to live fully in the present moment, trusting wholeheartedly in God's perfect timing and unwavering promises. By releasing our own agendas and aligning our thoughts with His divine will, we activate the dynamic laws that manifest our deepest desires. This active trust is not about passive waiting but about engaging confidently with God's plan, sowing seeds of NOW faith, and nurturing them with patience and obedience. As we master the art of maintaining NOW faith, we unlock the door to profound personal and spiritual growth, witnessing firsthand how this immediate, unshakable faith reshapes our reality and leads us into a life overflowing with blessings and fulfillment.

| 11 |

The Magnetic Power of
Thought Attract Your Desires

*D*iscover how your Subconscious Mind's thought frequency attracts like matter and shapes the reality of your accepted images, whether good or whether bad.

In the quiet recesses of our minds lies a magnetic force—an unseen power that shapes our realities and attracts the experiences we manifest. Every thought we entertain sends out ripples into the universe, resonating at frequencies that align with like matter. This process, though often unconscious, is the very essence of the Dynamic Law of Attraction. By understanding how our subconscious mind operates, we can learn to harness this power to draw into our lives the blessings and opportunities that reflect our innermost desires. Yet, we must also recognize that this same force can bring forth challenges and obstacles if we allow negative thoughts to take root. The key lies in becoming aware of our thought patterns and intentionally cultivating a mindset that aligns with our highest aspirations.

It cannot be said too many times that the mind is the fertile ground where the seeds of destiny are sown. Every thought we entertain is a seed with the potential to grow and shape the course of our lives. Just as a gardener cultivates the soil to produce a bountiful harvest, we must tend to our minds with care and intentionality. The quality of our thoughts determines the quality of our lives; they are the blueprint from which our reality is constructed.

Consider the immense power that resides within a single thought. It can ignite a vision, spark a revolution, or transform a life. Our thoughts influence our emotions, guide our decisions, and ultimately define our character. By gaining control over our thought patterns, we unlock the ability to direct our paths toward the fulfillment of our deepest desires and God-given purpose.

Yet, many of us drift through life unaware of the thoughts that dominate our minds. We allow negativity, doubt, and fear to take root, unaware of the detrimental harvest they will yield. It's time to awaken to the realization that we are not passive recipients of life's circumstances but active participants in creating our reality. Through conscious and deliberate thinking, aligned with divine principles, we can manifest a destiny that reflects our highest aspirations.

This transformative journey begins with acknowledging that every thought is a choice. We have the authority to accept thoughts that empower us and reject those that hinder us. By aligning our minds with truths that uplift and inspire, we set in motion the dynamic laws that bring our desires into existence. As the Apostle Paul reminds us:

"Be not deceived, God is not mocked, whatsoever a man sows, that shall he reap." (Galatians 6:7 KJV)

Everything that exists in our world originated as a thought. Every remarkable invention, groundbreaking discovery, and profound transformation first took shape in the fertile landscape of the mind before it could find its expression in the physical realm. At the heart of this process lies the Subconscious Mind, a silent yet powerful engine that drives our experiences. It diligently acts upon every deliberate thought we plant within it, sculpting our lives according to the essence of those thoughts. Importantly, the Subconscious Mind does not discern between what is deemed good or bad, positive or negative; it simply responds to the seeds we nurture within it. This reality underscores the necessity of being intentional about what we permit into our Conscious Mind, for it is this very input that ultimately determines the harvest our Subconscious will yield.

Your life is a direct reflection of your most dominant thoughts. Whether you're aware of it or not, your beliefs shape your experiences. To see transformation, you must take responsibility for the thoughts you entertain. It's not enough to avoid negative thinking—you must actively sow positive, faith-filled thoughts if you expect to see a harvest of success and abundance. Your thoughts are the most powerful tool you possess in shaping your reality. Take conscious control of what you allow to take root in your Subconscious Mind, by doing so your life will reflect the success and abundance of your desires.

A mind burdened by indecision, caught in the struggle between "to do" and "not to do," becomes unstable and restless. This absence of clarity can significantly hinder the power of the Subconscious Mind, which functions much like a fertile garden that requires a clear vision for effective cultivation. To unlock its full potential, you must take charge of your thoughts and harness the transformative power that enables you to create the life you desire. Once your aspirations are firmly embedded within your Subconscious, it springs into action, diligently working to manifest your destined reality.

If you aspire to achieve a specific level of wealth or income, it is essential to be both assured and fully convinced that the dynamic laws of creation are poised to bring your desire into reality. Once you have embraced this image as the solution to your request, released your words into the Mind of Christ with unwavering NOW faith, and believed without doubt, the Subconscious Mind has no other role than to receive and manifest the image you have implanted within it. In this transformative process, the act of "speaking the word" becomes a vital component of creation. To "speak the word" is to align yourself with God's divine creative power, proclaiming His promises over your life with authority, conviction, and deep NOW faith.

As 1 Peter 4:11 says, *"If any man speak, let him speak as the oracles of God."* When you speak with the authority of God's Word—fully trusting in His promises—you activate a divine power that can transform your desires into tangible reality. This dynamic interaction creates the ideal conditions for success, abundance, health, and any other blessings you seek. As you express your words infused with NOW faith, you release the creative force of God that flows in and through you. Therefore, it is crucial to stop tormenting yourself with regret or indecision. Once you have experienced cleansing and forgiveness, your responsibility is to speak with unwavering authority and to act with NOW faith. In doing so, you empower the Subconscious Mind to manifest the positive seeds you diligently plant, allowing your life to flourish in alignment with divine purpose.

The power of thought, followed closely by the spoken word, has always represented the initial step in the process of creation. This profound concept is of immense significance, as it reflects God's divine pattern of creation. The potency of the word is such that nothing can withstand it when spoken with unwavering conviction. As the Scriptures proclaim, *"For the word of God is quick, and powerful, and sharper than any two-edged sword, piercing even to the dividing asunder of soul and spirit, and of the joints and marrow, and a discerner of the thoughts and intent of the HEART"* (Hebrews 4:12 KJV). In the book of Genesis, we witness God's creative power at work: *"And God said, 'Let there be light,' and there was light"* (Genesis 1:3). In much the same way, our words possess inherent power—not because we are divine in our own right, but because we are made in God's image and entrusted with dominion over the earth. Our spoken words, therefore, are tools for manifestation that can shape the reality around us.

However, speaking with conviction does not imply forcing our will upon the world or attempting to control outcomes. The dynamic Law of Creation works not by human force or sheer willpower, but by alignment with God's will and a mindset of acceptance joined with the Mind of Christ. In Hebrews 4:12, we are reminded of the power of God's word—it discerns, divides, and pierces into the very heart of our being, including our Subconscious Mind. Just as the Subconscious Mind acts on what is planted, so does the Word of God operate with dynamic and eternal power, bringing forth fruit from the seeds planted by NOW faith.

The Dynamic Law of Attraction is the law of the manifestation of beliefs, thoughts, words, and desires. The method by which this Dynamic Law may be controlled so as to produce only good is by you refusing to accept evil. A word to the farmer: Weed out evil streaming thoughts by recognizing they are in disobedience to the Mind of Christ. Weeding brings them to obedience by casting them out of your stream. When you have envisioned a goal and created its attainment on the plane of the mind, nothing can stop you from realizing that goal but the creation of your failure on the same plane of mind. This is why an architect first plans the building the builder will build prior to construction.

The Subconscious Mind is a brilliant, intuitive discerner. Given a premise like, "I will create a great company", it can produce a series of brilliant, visionary and logical steps for the accomplishment of its attainment. The power into which you project your thoughts is a subconscious realm, the creative force that builds and constructs all form and circumstance. But it is done according to how you think. Now it is impossible for you to MAKE this power do anything. You cannot, by sheer force of WILL, bend this power to suit your needs. You are not greater than God.

You cannot either stop or start this power in its creating; for it is greater than you are and moves according to dynamic law. You cannot say, "I'm going to create a great company", with all the determination and ferociousness you can muster and expect that you are creating, in your experience, anything other than belligerence, disobedience, and opposition to God's will. *"Now listen, you who say, today or tomorrow, we will go to this or to that city, spend a year there, carry on business and make money. why you did not even know what will happen tomorrow. What is your life? You are a mist that appears for a little while and then vanishes. Instead, you ought to say, "If it is the Lord's will, we will live and do this or that." As it is, you boast in your arrogant schemes. All such boasting is evil."* (James 4:13-16 NIV)

You must embrace acceptance rather than demand. It is crucial never to attempt to WILL anything into existence physically. All your efforts to WILL for money will yield nothing, as that represents a misapplication of dynamic law. Money will be created in your experience only if you realize and know that there is an abundance all about you and you accept it. In other words, you don't demand money through popular Christian affirmations like "Money Cometh" or "I am money." You cannot force money into your life while harboring the belief that there is a scarcity and that you lack sufficient funds. Instead, you should accept that there is great abundance available to you, and you must KNOW this truth. This understanding embodies the proper use of dynamic law, contrasting sharply with the misguided exercise of individual will. For the force of your will against the will of God must inevitably set up that same thing in your experience, so that you see opposition instead of cooperation. Recognizing the abundance around you allows you to align with divine flow, inviting prosperity into your reality.

Embrace the power of expectation and acceptance; understand and immerse yourself in the experience; cultivate a spirit of positivity and gratitude. The magnificent Dynamic Law of Attraction and the principles of creation operate as profound laws of attunement, revealing their wonders only to those who approach with gentle curiosity, not to those who bang relentlessly at the door with force. What is truly required is a childlike faith—an unwavering NOW faith that opens the heart and mind to infinite possibilities. Like a child, we must trust that all good flows effortlessly into our lives, as if it were the most natural occurrence. They innately believe that their heartfelt desires are not only heard but are already being guided toward them by a loving Everlasting Father. Let us, too, embrace this innocent NOW faith and allow it to lead us to the abundance that awaits.

Expect, know, and accept with unwavering NOW Faith and belief. These are the secret keys that unlock the power of your prayer and meditation. You cannot attain the necessary attunement or effectively respond to divine guidance when you are consciously pounding at the door of heaven, desperately trying to force something into existence or prevent something from occurring in the physical realm. You may declare, "This is not the will of God for my life!" But how can you truly know? When have you taken the time to attune yourself to God and ask why you find yourself in a small apartment instead of the home you desire? It is in moments of stillness and reflection that you gain insight into God's plans for you, allowing you to align your desires with His divine purpose. Rather than demanding change, approach your situation with a heart open to understanding, and you will begin to see the greater possibilities that await you.

Just because you feel the lust of your eyes or envy someone who has manifested their desires, does that truly indicate that it is God's will for you to have those things right now? Many women have unwittingly placed unnecessary pressure on their household finances and their husband's ability to provide, often stemming from a lack of attunement and divine guidance in their pursuits. As the Scriptures remind us, *"The wise woman builds her house, but with her own hands the foolish one tears hers down"* (Proverbs 14:1 NIV). This verse highlights the importance of wisdom and discernment in creating a nurturing environment. Instead of succumbing to envy or desire, seek God's guidance and allow His wisdom to direct your path. When you align your aspirations with divine purpose, you cultivate a solid foundation for your home and relationships, leading to true abundance and fulfillment.

Without sowing a seed, there can be no harvest. God will not violate His own dynamic laws, nor will He disregard His established system of seed time and harvest time. As the Scriptures remind us, *"God will not be mocked..."* This profound truth emphasizes that you cannot willfully obtain what you have not sown for, plain and simple. Every time you consume what you have not planted, you are engaging in an act of theft or borrowing against your future harvest—a debt that you must be prepared to repay or relinquish.

It is essential to understand that the principle of sowing and reaping is foundational to the abundance you seek. Each seed you plant—whether through your thoughts, actions, or words—determines the nature of the harvest you will eventually reap. Therefore, approach your desires with a heart willing to invest in the right seeds, nurturing them with NOW faith and intention. By doing so, you align yourself with divine principles, ensuring that your harvest will be plentiful and fulfilling in accordance with God's perfect timing.

This message is for those who believe they can simply "name it and claim it" through a forceful declaration of confessions or affirmations. It is as though you are attempting to compel God to align His will with your own desires and statements. The notion of imposing your will upon God's divine purpose is neither justifiable nor valid.

When you fully accept the power of Almighty God as greater than yourself, you come to understand that He will create in your experience only that which you genuinely believe—this is the act of sowing seeds of NOW faith. Furthermore, you will discover that He will provide the answers to your questions and fulfill your desires—this is the process of reaping your harvest. To achieve this, you must release your need to control your circumstances and the challenges you face. Instead, accept God's response, which is often manifested in the form of a clear image or vision. By doing so, you open yourself up to His divine guidance and allow His perfect will to unfold in your life.

As we journey forward, let us hold fast to the understanding that our thoughts are the architects of our destiny. By gaining control over our minds and intentionally sowing seeds of positivity, NOW faith, and purpose, we harness the incredible power within us to manifest the reality we desire. Challenges and obstacles may arise, but these are not setbacks; they are opportunities for growth and refinement. Embrace them with a grateful heart, knowing that each trial strengthens your NOW faith and shapes your character. Remember, it is through perseverance and unwavering belief that we achieve completeness and fulfillment.

| 12 |

NOW Faith Speaks & Action Aligns with Your Words

*E*xplore *the profound connection between belief, spoken word, dynamic law, and action as the ultimate gateway - paving the way for miracles and manifestation that unlocks God's promises of abundance into the life you envision.*

NOW faith is not passive; it is alive and dynamic. The words we speak, infused with belief, carry the seeds of manifestation. However, it is not enough to merely speak—action is required to bring NOW faith into full expression. When we take intentional steps in alignment with our NOW faith, we activate the dynamic laws of divine creation, proving our trust in God's promises. This chapter explores the essential relationship between words, belief, and the movement required that draws miracles into our lives. Your actions become the bridge between the spiritual and the material, opening the door for abundance and fulfillment through divine order. A compelling example of NOW faith in action is found in (Acts 3:1-10 NLT):

"One day Peter and John went to the Temple at three o'clock in the afternoon, the hour for prayer. There at the Beautiful Gate, as it was called, was a man who had been lame all his life. Every day he was carried to the gate to beg for money from the people who were going into the Tem-

ple. When he saw Peter and John going in, he begged them to give him
something. They looked straight at him, and Peter said, "Look at us!" So he
looked at them, expecting to get something from them. But Peter said to
him, "I have no money at all, but I give you what I have: in the name of Je-
sus Christ of Nazareth I order you to get up and walk!" Then he took him
by his right hand and helped him up. At once the man's feet and ankles be-
came strong; he jumped up, stood on his feet, and started walking around.
Then he went into the Temple with them, walking and jumping and prais-
ing God. The people there saw him walking and praising God, and when
they recognized him as the beggar who had sat at the Beautiful Gate, they
were all surprised and amazed at what had happened to him."

In this miraculous account from Acts, we see not only the power of NOW faith in action but also the perfect alignment of the disciples' will with the will of God. Peter and John, filled with unwavering belief in the name of Jesus, spoke with divine authority. Their words were not spoken in isolation but in full alignment with God's timing and purpose for this man's healing. It was God's will that on this very day, the man be restored, and in that moment, the Laws of Attraction and Creation were activated. As Peter spoke, dynamic NOW faith called physical restoration into being, and the atoms within the man's feet and ankles responded to the power of God's word through Peter. The divine intelligence within the man's body recognized the command in NOW faith, demonstrating the interconnectedness of belief, thought, action, and matter.

When Peter and John took the man by the hand to help him up, it was a physical act that mirrored the spiritual reality already set in motion. Their action aligned perfectly with God's will, releasing divine power to manifest healing in an instant. The Law of Attraction drew forth the atoms of healing and restoration, causing them to move in harmony with God's will. In this moment, human NOW faith and divine intervention came together, and the man was fully healed, demonstrating the miraculous results that come when our words, actions, and will are fully aligned with God's perfect plan.

Thomas Edison, the famed inventor, was deeply preoccupied with what he termed "the obvious choice of the atom" in its infinite acceptances and rejections within chemical combinations. When two chemicals are mixed, certain atoms combine while others do not. Edison pondered why specific atoms would choose to bond with certain others. The only conceivable answer was that atoms possess a conscious choice in whether they combine with other atoms. While Edison did not suggest that atoms have self-awareness, he recognized the intelligence or consciousness inherent in them—the ability to make choices.

This concept is beautifully illustrated in the story of Peter and John and the man at the gate Beautiful. The atoms forming the mass of the man's feet and ankles "chose" to be attracted to the atoms of the rest of his body were diving healing could take place. Through the Mind of Christ, Peter and John received divine guidance on how to activate this atomic attraction. The atoms, as centers of force, responded to the belief, spiritual command and action, showcasing that matter is not passive but responsive to divine intention.

These dynamic immutable laws respond to faith-filled thoughts aligned with God's will. By understanding the consciousness inherent in all things and the power of our minds, we can engage with the Dynamic Law of Attraction to manifest God's promises. The miracle at the gate called Beautiful was not a mere historical event but a demonstration of what is possible when one operates in alignment with divine laws.

In view of this very busy universe of ours, perhaps it seems strange that you are told that the path to power and accomplishment lies in getting your physical body quiet and working only with your mind.

Do not burden your mind with what actions you should take. Action happens naturally as a response to thought. Life and movement are synonymous. Concern yourself rather with guidance for your movement and action. Action governed solely by stimuli received from the outer world is false action and can result in nothing other than the frustration of your desires.

The appearance of delayed answers to prayers, confessions, and affirmations often leads to frustration, especially when unguided actions are taken. Take, for instance, when you pray for a new car. The next day, filled with impatience, you visit five car lots, hear "No" four times, and finally get a "Yes" that locks you into a bad loan. This is a prime example of dissipating your energy by treating obstacles or circumstances as purely physical things to overcome. No one, by their own strength, is capable of forcing their way through these situations. Man is not big enough to achieve anything alone—he must recognize the greater power at work in the universe. Everywhere he looks, there is evidence of God's dynamic force. And this power cannot be fought or manipulated. Instead, one must attune themselves to God's will and work in harmony with it. Only then will answers and blessings manifest in alignment with divine timing and purpose.

The man who walks in step with God moves in divine power, and his actions carry supernatural reward. What others struggle to achieve in a year, those aligned with God's will can accomplish in an hour. Yet it is not through their own effort or busyness, but rather because their activity is guided, purposeful, and infused with the strength of the Almighty. Their objectives are directed by the limitless resources and power of the Subconscious Mind, which operates in perfect harmony with the Mind of Christ. For such men, lack, limitation, failure, and disease are nearly incomprehensible. They don't dwell on these things because they are attuned to the abundance and victory that flows from walking with God. What others perceive as obstacles, they view as opportunities for divine manifestation, scarcely aware of anything but God's sufficiency.

Know that every idea produces itself on the physical plane, is in effect exactly like the cause. Place no limits on your thinking. All things are possible with Christ. The moment they are considered probable, they become certainty. "I can do all things through Christ which strengtheneth me." (Philippians 4:13 KJV)

| 13 |

The Genesis of Sound: The Blueprint of All Matter

*G*et ready to be amazed as you unlock the mystery of how sound energy *forms every atom of the universe and becomes Matter — and how tapping into this dynamic law will align your words with God's creative power to shape your destiny.*

Ever wonder what really holds the world together? Dive deeper into the mystery of creation and discover how this profound truth unlocks the potential for miracles and manifestation in your life. Beneath the surface of what we see lies a hidden force—sound. This invisible yet powerful energy returns to its source, transforming into the very building blocks of reality. In this chapter, you'll uncover the divine connection between your words, God's voice, and how these forces shape the physical world around you.

Our limited Conscious Mind, deeply rooted in the carnal, flesh-driven nature, plays a convincing trick on us every day. It classifies and analyzes every experience, constantly sorting through sensations of pain and pleasure, ultimately prioritizing survival over spiritual truth. This thought process, lodged within the brain, tirelessly weighs, measures, and categorizes everything it encounters, reinforcing the illusion that the physical world is all there is. But this could not be further from the truth. The Conscious Mind, with its limited understanding, seeks to trap us in the belief that what we see is the ultimate reality. However, as you'll learn, it is the sound of creation and the divine frequencies within that are the true forces shaping the universe. It is time to break free from the limitations of the Sarx flesh and tap into the spiritual power that has been working beneath the surface all along.

When you realize that sound is not just a vibration, but a force connected to the Creator's voice, you begin to see how your words can align with God's will. This shift in understanding will allow you to wield the power of sound to manifest miracles in your life. The key is in the unseen, in the connection between sound, spirit, and the physical world.

Consider the chair upon which you now sit. It feels solid and dependable, yet it's nothing more than a collection of rapidly moving atoms, akin to a high-speed train zipping through a city. The reality is that 99.9% of what you're sitting on is empty space, with only the tiniest fraction made of actual mass. If you stop to reflect on this, you'll feel as though you're sitting on nothing. But here's the remarkable truth—your body is made of the same Matter, all moving in constant motion, separated by vast amounts of space. The only difference between you and the chair is your form and consciousness. Both you and that chair are composed of the same fundamental substance: atoms, molecules, Matter bound together by forces of nature.

For many years, scientists believed the atom to be the smallest indivisible unit of matter. It was thought to be the building block of everything—until they discovered that atoms were themselves composed of even smaller particles, such as electrons, protons, and neutrons. Inside this microscopic universe, protons and electrons orbit like planets around the sun, held together by the strong nuclear force. When speculation arose as to whether these subatomic particles could be split, the consequences were monumental. On August 6th, 1945, over Hiroshima, Japan, that speculation became devastating reality. When the atom was split, the nuclear forces holding it together were released, creating a massive explosion of energy—an event that forever changed our understanding of Matter and energy.

When an atom is split, the element disintegrates, but what's truly fascinating is what happens next. Though invisible to the naked eye, you can hear the sound of energy returning to its source. This revelation leads us to a powerful truth: the very essence of the atom, and indeed all Matter, is energy. At its core, sound energy forms the foundation of all creation. This understanding takes us back to Genesis 1, where God's spoken word initiated creation: "And God said... and it was." The sound of His words unleashed the forces that formed atoms, drawing electrons, protons, and neutrons together, shaping vibrating Matter into existence by His verbal command.

In scientific terms, mass is potential energy, and energy is potential mass, as demonstrated by Einstein's famous equation $E=mc^2$. This principle shows that a certain mass can be converted into an equivalent amount of energy, and vice versa. For example, a small amount of uranium can unleash immense energy, while energy can also create Matter under the right conditions. Both mass and energy originate from one fundamental source, eternal and ever-present, infinite in its nature. It exists beyond the constraints of time and space, manifesting in both the physical and spiritual realms. This energy is the true substance behind all things, and it holds the key to understanding not only the universe but the essence of our very existence.

The physical world, as you perceive it, cannot possibly provide the ultimate answer to your existence. The key to that understanding lies elsewhere, beyond what your conscious, finite mind can grasp. You must reach deep into your spirit, through the mind of your heart, where the Everlasting Counselor resides, waiting to provide answers that cannot be found in the material world. It is not through reasoning or deduction, but through a divine connection, that these answers are revealed. As the Word says, *"If any of you lacks wisdom, you should ask God, who gives generously to all without finding fault, and it will be given to you. But when you ask, you must believe and not doubt, because the one who doubts is like a wave of the sea, blown and tossed by the wind. That person should not expect to receive anything from the Lord. Such a person is double-minded and unstable in all they do."* (James 1:5-8, NIV). NOW faith is the anchor that aligns us with divine wisdom.

Matter and energy are not separate entities—they are one and the same, expressions of a single infinite creative substance. This infinite energy is the source of all intelligent design, and intelligent design, by nature, comes from an intelligent designer. When we perceive this energy in its purest form, it returns to the source as invisible power, beyond the reach of our five senses. The Conscious Mind, limited by its fleshly boundaries, cannot fully comprehend this. Instead, it is through the spirit of man, seated in the Subconscious Mind, that we begin to grasp this source—not by logic, but by revelation. This revelation is a Spirit-to-spirit communication, transmitted on a frequency the Conscious Mind cannot detect. We don't "find" God; He reveals Himself to those who are His. As it is written, *"All things are delivered unto me of my Father: and no man knoweth the Son, but the Father; neither knoweth any man the Father, save the Son, and he to whomsoever the Son will reveal Him."* (Matthew 11:27, KJV).

When Simon Peter recognized Jesus as the Christ, it wasn't through intellect or human understanding but through divine revelation. As Jesus told him, *"Blessed art thou, Simon Bar-jona: for flesh and blood hath not revealed it unto thee, but my Father which is in heaven."* (Matthew 16:17, KJV). The deeper truths, the ones that shape our understanding of reality, are not figured out—they are revealed. These revelations come not from the physical world or through human effort, but from God Himself, directly into the spirit of man, guiding those who seek Him with a pure heart.

Everything in existence is fundamentally one mass, a substance without beginning or end, without past or future, existing only in the eternal now. Einstein famously said that mass traveling at the speed of light would appear to be everywhere at once, suggesting that the speed of light represents infinity. This concept is but a fragment of the master mathematician's Theory of Relativity, a theory he claimed came to him not through calculation, but through intuition—as a revelation. The scriptures echo this truth, declaring the eternal nature of God: *"Look, he is coming with the clouds, and every eye will see him, even those who pierced him, and all the peoples on earth will mourn because of him. So shall it be! Amen. 'I am the Alpha and the Omega,' says the Lord God, 'who is, and who was, and who is to come, the Almighty'"* (Revelation 1:7-8, NIV). What Einstein perceived scientifically, God declared through His Word—eternity, the infinite now.

As far as the eye can see, the mind projects, and the spirit perceives, there is nothing but Dynamic Immutable Law. When man examines the smallest units of matter he can visualize, the atom, he finds a nucleus surrounded by moving parts in constant, never-ending motion. Similarly, when he looks to the largest units he can perceive, the Solar System, he again finds a nucleus—our sun—around which planets and other celestial bodies orbit, in constant, unceasing motion. The pattern repeats, revealing a divine order in both the microcosm and macrocosm.

How remarkable it is that the smallest and largest units of matter we know share the same fundamental structure! The atom, a universe unto itself, may contain even smaller worlds, just as our universe could be part of an infinitely larger system. It is humbling to consider how small and insignificant we seem when we contemplate the vastness of infinity. Yet, in all this boundless expanse, we find that our perceptions—our thoughts, our observations—exist within the mind. And in that mind, with all its limitations, we often place ourselves vainly at the center of the universe, forgetting the greater truth: that God alone is the true center, the Alpha and Omega, the source and sustainer of all that is.

Let's take, for example, that chair mentioned earlier that you may be still sitting in right now. Again, it's composed entirely of energy, constantly in motion. But the vain Conscious Mind will protest: No! It's solid. I can feel it, it's hard. It has a specific shape and color, and it's real. I can leave it today and it will still be here tomorrow. It can't move by itself—only I, or someone else capable of moving it, can shift it. It's not alive; it's inanimate. It's a chair, and I know what a chair is! This is the typical reasoning of the Conscious Mind, operating in the Sarx, clinging to the tangible and visible. We've been trained to view the physical world as the ultimate reality. Yet, until you switch frequencies from the Sarx to the Spirit, from AM to FM, this narrow perspective will keep you grounded, operating as a mere mortal, disconnected from the divine truth of creation.

Now, this doesn't mean we should ignore the physical world, pretend the flesh doesn't exist, or try to walk through the chair as if it's not there. If you try that, you'll get a hard knock or a quick fall! What this means is that physical objects and circumstances are not the final reality. As the scripture says, *"For we fix our attention, not on things that are seen, but on things that are unseen. What can be seen lasts only for a time, but what cannot be seen lasts forever"* (2 Corinthians 4:18, GNT). Faith opens our eyes to understand that *"the universe was created by God's word, so that what can be seen was made out of what cannot be seen"* (Hebrews 11:3, GNT). The true essence of reality lies beyond what the eye can perceive.

The entire universe is framed by intentional design, spoken into existence by the mighty words of God. It wasn't a random accident, and neither are you. Man was not an accident. Consider the analogy from British astronomer Sir Fred Hoyle, who criticized the idea of life arising purely by chance. Hoyle famously likened the probability of life forming randomly to a tornado sweeping through a junkyard and assembling a fully functioning Boeing 747 from scattered parts. His point? Complex systems like life don't just happen by accident. They require a guiding intelligence, a designer. In the same way, your existence is part of a divine plan, not the result of random events.

"Then God said, 'And now we will make human beings; they will be like us and resemble us. They will have power over the fish, the birds, and all animals, domestic and wild, large and small'" (Genesis 1:26, GNT). You are woven into the fabric of this great design, just as every other element of creation fits perfectly into its intended place. The complexity and detail behind life, the universe, and all existence point to an intelligence of infinite scope and power—God Himself, the ultimate creator.

God's plan for humanity was not only intentional but empowering. *"So God created human beings, making them to be like Himself. He created them male and female, blessed them, and said, 'Have many children, so that your descendants will live all over the earth and bring it under their control. I am putting you in charge of the fish, the birds, and all the wild animals. I have provided all kinds of grain and all kinds of fruit for you to eat; but for all the wild animals and for all the birds I have provided grass and leafy plants for food'—and it was done"* (Genesis 1:27-30, GNT). You, as part of this divine design, were created with purpose, to reflect God's image and to steward the earth with wisdom and care.

What a towering and wondrous world we live in! We can call upon the power of the Everlasting Father, the Creator of all, through the simplicity of meditation, praise, prayer, and thought, through NOW faith and conviction. A direct line, connecting us to the divine through a frequency born of Spirit. Nothing is impossible for man, for the Creator dwells within us and gives us all we can visualize, believe, and ask for through the Mind of Christ. This is the very essence of divine connection, where thought and NOW faith align to create reality.

But we must not allow the Conscious Mind to deceive us into believing that the physical world is the ultimate reality. We cannot afford to spend our days following the dictates of the fleshly Conscious Mind as if it were the highest plane of existence. This Sarx mind, bound to the physical, is but a machine for dealing with pain and pleasure, incapable of discerning spiritual truth. Instead, we must constantly reach within, to connect with the Wonderful Counselor, the Holy Spirit of Truth, given to us by grace. It is through this connection that we realize all form and Matter begin as thoughts, that the first cause of all unseen creation is birthed by thought, spoken into existence through words of NOW faith and conviction, and then manifested by our acceptance and expectation.

We must understand that we can contact our Everlasting Father for answers to all of life's problems. We are the creators of our own circumstances, giving birth to them in the womb of our minds. Nothing in the universe can stop our thoughts from becoming reality, for this is the Law and Dynamics of Life that God blessed us with in the beginning. When creation is clear and born of NOW faith and conviction, nothing can hinder that image from becoming real. Once this vision is planted in your mind and accepted in your spirit, you have completed all that is required of you. The process of creation—seed time and harvest time, place and circumstance—must be left to the Subconscious Mind, which seeks out the "how to's" from the Wonderful Counselor. One day, He will drop the image into your spirit, and its final fulfillment will be at hand.

The physical Matter you desire may come from a direction you expect, or it may manifest in ways you've never imagined. But don't strain, urge, or become impatient. Simply hold onto NOW faith and let go. Remember, when you observe too closely or anxiously, doubt creeps in. You've already done your part by creating the mental image with complete NOW faith, and with that act, the process is finished. Be assured that the image will become real in your physical world, for you are dealing with Dynamic Law—unchanging, unstoppable.

As the scripture says, *"Therefore I say unto you, Take no thought for your life, what ye shall eat, or what ye shall drink; nor yet for your body, what ye shall put on. Is not the life more than meat, and the body than raiment?... Therefore take no thought, saying, What shall we eat? or, What shall we drink? or, Wherewithal shall we be clothed?... But seek ye first the kingdom of God, [God's way of doing and being], and his righteousness [right standing]; and all these things shall be added unto you"* (Matthew 6:25, 31, 33 AMP). All things come from the same source, and just as they are of one source, so too are objects and circumstances. These exist as the result of the heart and mind's desire, projected through the subconscious into the infinite creative power of the One Mighty Source of which we are all a part.

Thought is the only mover. You will receive only what you are capable of conceiving. Whatever you conceive, that will be added unto you. If doubt and fear dominate your thinking, those very things you fear will be upon you, for they are very real images and stronger convictions to you that the Subconscious Mind and the Mind of Christ will create into your reality. Therefore, guard your thoughts, align them with NOW faith, and let your desires be guided by the Spirit, for all things flow from this source.

Let's examine the path of Job's own thoughts and words, which turned into Strongholds, and put these laws to the test. Job, in his daily practice, consistently worried about his children: *"When a period of feasting had run its course, Job would make arrangements for them* [his children] *to be purified. Early in the morning he would sacrifice a burnt of-*

fering for each of them, thinking (thoughts attract), *'Perhaps my children have sinned and cursed God in their hearts.'"* This was not a fleeting concern but a Stronghold in his mind — *"This was Job's regular custom"* (Job 1:5, NIV). His fear-filled prayer life became habitual, rooted deeply in his spirit, and created a Stronghold—a constant fear of what might happen.

What was the result of Job's continual prayers, motivated by fear rather than NOW faith? *"While he was still speaking, yet another messenger came and said, 'Your sons and daughters were feasting and drinking wine at the oldest brother's house, when suddenly a mighty wind swept in from the desert and struck the four corners of the house. It collapsed on them, and they are dead, and I am the only one who escaped to tell you!'"* (Job 1:18-19, NIV). The very thing Job feared—his Stronghold—manifested in his life. When the tragedy struck, Job's response was clear: *"What I feared has come upon me; what I dreaded has happened to me"* (Job 3:25, NIV). In other words, *"My Stronghold has come upon me; that dreaded fear I carried has manifested."* Job's continual fearful thoughts, which he reinforced with his daily prayers, became his reality.

Job's story has often been portrayed as a cosmic bet between God and Satan, but there is a deeper truth at play. The scripture tells us, *"God is not a man that He should lie, nor the Son of Man that He should repent"* (Numbers 23:19, NIV). So how do we frame the conversation between God and Satan regarding Job? God did not place Job in Satan's hands out of a bet; instead, God revealed the truth of Job's situation. God essentially says, *"Has my son Job considered his own thoughts and fears? His habitual fear has opened the door for the enemy to enter his life. Job's thought life has attracted the very thing he feared."* God was simply affirming what was already true: Job's fearful thoughts had given Satan access to him. Yet, in His mercy, God commanded Satan, *"Do not kill him; that is not authorized"* (Job 2:6, paraphrased).

The Law of Attraction is automatic, just like gravity. What are your prayers attracting into your life that you may be blaming God for? God needs your NOW faith to move into action—faith is the currency of heaven. But Satan needs your [NOW] fear to move into your life situations, and fear is the currency of hell. When you pray, the scripture instructs us to pray in faith, believing that we have already received what we ask for, and God will grant the petitions of our hearts. However, praying the same prayer over and over again, day after day, turns faith into fear. Repeatedly asking for the same thing shifts your prayers from faith-based declarations to fear-based pleading, which no longer attracts heavenly answers but hellish manifestations.

We cannot escape living within the realm of the Subconscious Mind, nor can we escape the constant stream of thoughts that fill it. And just as Job's thoughts became his reality, so do ours. Yet, here lies our power: we can control our thoughts, and by controlling our thoughts, we can control our destinies. We hold within us the ability to be as great and powerful as we can conceive, for the very source of all creation—the Everlasting Father—dwells within us. That unlimited power, the Creator of the universe, is at our disposal.

"The universe hums like a great harp string
Resounding a mighty cord
Answering each thought by returning a thing
From the place where all things are stored."
-Anonymous Author-

Our foundation is simple: thoughts make things. To fully understand this profound truth, we must return to the origin of all form. When we break down substance, we find atoms; when we break down atoms, we unleash energy. This leads us to one conclusion: the foundation of all creation is unharnessed, invisible energy. But what is this energy, and where does it come from? It doesn't explode randomly through space but manifests in matter or motion, always following an intelligent design. This energy, while unseen, is first expressed in sound—returning to its source. Sound is the essence of all energy, the invisible force that speaks Matter into existence.

The flow of this energy, from the smallest atom to the largest solar system, follows a divine and intelligent plan, governed by Dynamic Immutable Laws of sound and action. These laws alone account for the attraction and accumulation of substance into form. Whether in the atom or the solar system, the same principles apply—sound and movement create order. The Solar System and the atom, though vastly different in scale, are identical in their construction. Both reveal the mind of the Architect, the Creator of all things.

"Let this mind be in you, which was also in Christ Jesus, who, being in the form of God, did not consider it robbery to be equal with God, but made Himself of no reputation, taking the form of a bondservant, and coming in the likeness of men." (Philippians 2:5-7 NKJV). This Mind of Christ, this spoken Word, is the first Dynamic Cause. This infinite plan, this energy, is the very substance from which all things were created. In the beginning was the Word, and through that Word, all creation came to be. *"All things were made through Him, and without Him, nothing was made that was made"* (John 1:3 NKJV).

"The Lord created me first of all, the first of his works, long ago. I was made in the very beginning, at the first, before the world began. I was born before the oceans, when there were no springs of water. I was born before the mountains, before the hills were set in place, before God made the earth and its fields or even the first handful of soil. I was there when he set the sky in place, when he stretched the horizon across the ocean, when he placed the clouds in the sky, when he opened the springs of the ocean and ordered the waters of the sea to rise no further than he said. I was there when he laid the earth's foundations. I was beside him like an architect, I was his daily

source of joy, always happy in his presence—happy with the world and pleased with the human race." (Proverbs 8:22-31 GNT)

This is the Immutable Dynamic Law of Creation—the infinite plan, the sound of the Word, and the Mind of Christ as the source and form of all Matter. In its purest form, Spirit energy—God's infinite presence—is expressed through intelligent sound and movement, brought forth by the Wonderful Counselor. It is through this sound, the Word of God, that all creation is directed, and it is by this Law that all prosperity and success flow. This divine order is the foundation upon which all of creation exists and thrives.

In God's grand design, each of us is called to form part of the Body of Christ, each according to the purpose for which we are anointed. Just as the natural body has one head, the spiritual body—the Body of Christ—has one head: Christ Himself. *"Now you are the body of Christ, and each one of you is a part of it"* (1 Corinthians 12:27 NIV). Christ, as the head of every man, operates through divine order: *"But I would have you know, that the head of every man is Christ; and the head of the woman is the man; and the head of Christ is God"* (1 Corinthians 11:3 KJV).

This Dynamic Law manifests itself through intelligent design at every level of creation. The first intelligent manifestation of the Wonderful Counselor appears as a center of force, represented by both the atom and the solar system. Nothing outside this Law calls these centers of force into being; rather, it is the nature of the Law to manifest them. The law is one of life, sound, movement, and energy, gathering into units of similar frequency in this vibrating universe.

To explore this further, envision all of space as a realm of pure vibration. These vibrations—rooted in intelligence—are the force that drives the universe. Different frequencies of vibration gather and form units of Matter. These units, whether atoms or entire solar systems, are brought into existence by the infinite Dynamic Law acting from within itself. The vibrations in pure universal subconscious intelligence are established at varying upper-range frequencies, and all vibrations of a similar frequency inevitably attract and form into Matter.

This process of creation is beautifully described in the Genesis account: *"In the beginning God created the heaven and the earth... and God said, Let there be light: and there was light"* (Genesis 1:1-3 KJV). Through His spoken Word, the Dynamic Law of Creation was set into motion, manifesting the heavens, the earth, and all living creatures. This same law is still in operation today, and just as it brought forth creation in Genesis, it continues to bring order, purpose, and life into existence.

| 14 |

Crush Doubt, Remove Strongholds & Unleash Victory

*D*iscover how embracing and planting the dynamic law of NOW faith in the fertile ground of your heart can break the strongholds of limitation and shatter the barriers of fear and doubt to unlock the divine abundance you desire.

Throughout our lives, we often find ourselves confined by the walls of our own making—barriers constructed from fear, doubt, and the limitations imposed by society. We tread familiar paths, comfortable in the known, yet deep within us stirs a yearning for something more. There's a whisper that tells us we were made for greater things, that beyond the horizons we see lies a realm of infinite possibilities waiting to be explored.

This whisper is the voice of God, inviting us to step beyond our self-imposed boundaries and into the vast expanse of His divine purpose. When we align our hearts and minds with His will, we tap into a source of limitless potential. It's like unlocking a hidden reservoir of strength, wisdom, and creativity that propels us toward destinies we never imagined.

Consider the heroes of faith who have gone before us—ordinary individuals who achieved extraordinary feats because they dared to believe in God's promises. They moved mountains, parted seas, and conquered giants not by their own might but through unwavering faith in the One who called them. Their lives testify to what is possible when we embrace God's infinite possibilities.

"Now faith is the substance of things hoped for, the evidence of things not seen. For by it the elders obtained a good report. Through faith we understand that the worlds were framed by the word of God, so that things which are seen were not made of things which do appear.

By faith Abel offered unto God a more excellent sacrifice than Cain, By faith Enoch was translated that he should not see death; By faith Noah, being warned of God of things not seen as yet, moved with fear, prepared an ark to the saving of his house; By faith Abraham, when he was called to go out into a place which he should after receive for an inheritance, obeyed; and he went out, not knowing whither he went; Through faith also Sara herself received strength to conceive seed, and was delivered of a child when she was past age, because she judged him faithful who had promised.

These all died in faith, not having received the promises, but having seen them afar off, and were persuaded of them, and embraced them, and confessed that they were strangers and pilgrims on the earth."
(Hebrews 11:1-13 Edited)

Yet, embracing this limitless potential requires us to relinquish control. It demands that we trust in God's plan over our own, acknowledging that His ways are higher than ours. It's a journey of NOW faith, where each step forward may not reveal the entire path but assures us of His guiding presence.

In our modern world, we often seek tangible keys to unlock success, happiness, or fulfillment. We strive for achievements that we believe will grant us control over our lives and futures. But true empowerment comes not from earthly attainments but from the spiritual keys that God offers—keys that unlock the mysteries of His kingdom and grant us access to His boundless resources.

Christ said He would give us the keys to the kingdom. A key unlocks something valuable, something unseen. Remembering how Thanos, the character in The Avengers, sought to control time, space and matter. He desired the capacity to not be bound by the constraints of time, like God and the host of the spiritual realm. His quest was to have all stones as one stone keeper—in other words, to possess all the keys to control time.

Thanos' primary motivation for collecting all six of the Infinity Stones was to eliminate half of all life in the universe. He believes that overpopulation leads to resource depletion, suffering, and eventual extinction of life due to scarce resources. By wiping out half of all living beings indiscriminately, he aims to restore balance and ensure a sustainable future for the survivors.

Thanos witnessed the downfall of his own planet, Titan, which collapsed under the weight of overpopulation and depleted resources. His proposal to save Titan by randomly eliminating half its population was rejected, leading to the planet's demise. This personal tragedy convinced him that drastic measures are necessary to prevent similar catastrophes elsewhere.

By obtaining all six Infinity Stones, Thanos gains the god-like power to instantly and efficiently carry out his plan on a universal scale with a snap of his fingers—an event referred to as "The Snap." He perceives his actions not as malevolent but as a merciful sacrifice for the greater good, believing that the ends justify the means. His conviction is so strong that he is willing to make personal sacrifices and endure opposition from others to achieve what he sees as a noble goal.

Although he had a lofty reason—to save the earth by eliminating half the population so the other half could survive—this would make him into a god to be served, pleaded with, and honored by those hoping to be among the surviving half. This is too much power for one man. Such a pursuit of power is a work of the flesh (Sarx), one that can only be satisfied by much sin in the process. He could not come out of that clean. Thanos did not create any of the human beings on his hit list. He had no orders from God or heaven that put him on that path. There is no scripture in the Holy Bible that permits or suggests that the earth could not sustain itself. In fact, the very idea that wiping out half the population might be the self-inflicted wound that causes the demise of the earth is paradoxical. You see, within that half could very well be the one person who holds the key to saving the world.

"I will give you the keys of the kingdom of heaven; whatever you bind on earth will be bound in heaven, and whatever you loose on earth will be loosed in heaven." Matthew 16:19 (NIV)

God has given "the key" of keys, the Matter Miner, to solve the perceived problem. God said this world would always have seedtime and harvest as long as it exists. Thanos got exactly what he projected from his Subconscious Mind to God. However, with just one Infinity Stone—one key, his key—he would have had the potential to solve the problem by seeking the Wonderful Counselor in NOW faith and waiting for the image of what his one key could do to assist, rather than attempting to do it all as a "go-getter." He should have yielded to the Spirit of Creation in using the one key (stone) he was given; the image of saving the world was already in his spirit.

This is similar to when John the Baptist was given "a key"—the key to proclaim in his ministry the coming of the Savior to the world. That one key, that one ministry, was his purpose. That purpose was the will of the Everlasting Father, as the plan was to bring forth the one true keeper of all the keys, whom He would task with giving them to those He found about the Father's business, mining matter. John's role was to prepare the people for the coming of the Messiah. He did this by telling people to repent, as the Kingdom of Heaven was near. Baptism was a Jewish ritual—people were totally immersed in water to symbolize cleansing. John's baptism was a symbol of repentance.

Once the Messiah arrived, the heavy lifting of John's ministry was complete. The key he had been given had unlocked the mystery of heaven and was no longer needed in the same way. The baptism portion, however, would have worked perfectly with the ministry of Jesus, had he chosen to close his operation and follow Jesus as His first disciple. He would have had the honor and kingdom work of baptizing the people set free by Jesus. Much like Thanos could have been a participant in God's plan and not simply a "go-getter." Many times, "go-getters" lose their heads.

This challenge is evident even among some of our contemporary pastors and spiritual leaders. Many have been entrusted with their divine key to preach, with the same unwavering focus and zeal as John the Baptist, staying true to the message God placed in their hearts. Yet, as the flock grows restless, developing "itchy ears" (2 Timothy 4:3), some leaders feel pressured to scratch those itches by delivering messages that stray from the key they were originally given. These altered sermons, once rooted in compromise, become entrenched thoughts and spiritual strongholds. And just as strongholds in the mind are difficult to dismantle, so too, once a leader begins catering to these misplaced desires, it becomes a challenge to return to the pure truth they were called to preach. It's a dangerous path, because once it begins, it's hard to stop—unless they return to the original mandate God placed in their hearts.

Every thought you entertain and accept becomes a seed planted within you, and like any seed, it will grow and ultimately produce a harvest in your physical reality. The choices you make begin in the Conscious Mind, but the acceptance of those choices—whether they are aligned with faith or fear—happens through the Subconscious Mind in the spirit. This is a sacred transaction, a spirit-to-Spirit transfer. When the Subconscious Mind operates on the divine frequency of the Mind of Christ, it activates the process of manifesting that accepted thought with NOW faith and unwavering conviction.

There are two frequencies at work within us: one, attuned to the physical world—the "Sarx"—that processes the five senses and wrestles with doubt and fear; the other, aligned with the matters of the spirit, processes through love, faith, and trust in God's promises. Understanding these two frequencies is critical, for it determines what you choose to manifest. When you choose faith and love, you operate in harmony with the divine, allowing the Mind of Christ to bring your desires into reality.

The Conscious Mind and the Subconscious Mind can be compared to software and the processing plant, each playing a vital role in shaping our reality. The Conscious Mind receives sensory input from the physical world, while the Subconscious Mind operates on a deeper, attunement-based discernment, aligning with the divine. Once you understand this, you will recognize that the apparent differences between you and anyone else are but an illusion. Your sense of self—your "I"—may have been conditioned by past experiences of lack and limitation. But when you cast out these imaginations, when you dethrone those false beliefs and establish your Positive Throne of Adam, renewing your mind to the knowledge of abundance, health, and divine provision, your "I" is transformed.

You may still occupy the same body, but the power of this inner transformation will soon manifest outwardly. As your consciousness shifts, so too will your surroundings. Your body will become energized, purposeful, free from fear, and aligned with the greatest force

168 - RAY WRIGHT JACOBS

in the universe—the dynamic power of God. This new vitality will reflect the truth that you are no longer the person of limitation, but one animated by the limitless power of the Spirit, operating in sync with the Mind of Christ.

As you close this journey through *Matter Miner*, understand this: the power to manifest, create, and thrive has always been within you, waiting to be unlocked. Every thought, every choice, every belief aligns with the frequency of the Mind of Christ, shaping the world around you in ways you may not yet fully comprehend. The limits you once believed in are but illusions, shattered by the truth of God's dynamic laws. Now, with your NOW faith activated and your will aligned, the universe itself responds to your vision, your NOW faith, and your conviction. What will you do with this knowledge? The next move is yours—there is no limit to where it may lead.

About the Author

Ray Wright Jacobs is a seasoned entrepreneur and visionary with over 29 years of experience in the real estate industry. Born with a passion for building and creating,

Ray became a licensed real estate agent in 1994 and advanced to a real estate broker by 1998. He founded and managed his own real estate brokerage, as well as a real estate development and investment companies, guiding numerous clients through the complexities of property transactions and investments.

As a husband, father of eleven and grandfather of seven, family has always been at the heart of Ray's journey. His personal life and professional endeavors are deeply intertwined, teaching him invaluable lessons about ambition, humility, and the true measures of success.

The real estate recession of 2007–2008 marked a pivotal point in Ray's life. Facing significant losses, he confronted the hard lessons of vanity and ego that had influenced his career. This period of reflection led him back to his first love: writing. Ray began channeling what he describes as "downloads from God," receiving profound insights and revelations that would shape his future work.

Drawing from these divine inspirations and the wisdom gleaned from hundreds of books read throughout his life, Ray authored *Matter Miner: Immutable Laws That Attract Success with Every Thought*. In this transformative book, he shares the dynamic universal laws that govern success, sharing with readers how to harness the power of their thoughts to manifest their deepest desires.

Ray's writing transcends conventional self-help literature by integrating spiritual insights with practical strategies. His unique perspective empowers individuals to align their minds with timeless truths, unlocking their potential to achieve lasting success and fulfillment.

Today, Ray Wright Jacobs continues to inspire and mentor others through his writing and speaking engagements. His commitment to personal growth and spiritual development serves as a guiding light for those seeking to navigate the complexities of life with wisdom and grace.

Appendix: Men's Hour of Intercessory Prayer

When asked how to pray for an hour as Jesus did, we find ourselves lost in vague requests, repetitive prayers and wish list loops. I prayed to God and asked Him to give me a way to be about His business and not mine. This is what He gave me to add to the 7-book series, The Remodel. I share this and challenge any man who wishes to cover his territory effectively to just read out loud and watch what happens:

ADAM = Authority Dominion And Might
MAN = God's Foundation of Creation – ADAM

CORPORATE INTERCESSION AND SPOKEN WARFARE OF GOD'S INTERCEEDING ROCKS, THE ADAM-MEN TO RE-VIVAL

1.) Thanksgiving   2.) Praise   3.) Petition
4.) Warfare   5.) Royal Decree   6.) Confession
7.) Rest-ord

Blessed art Thou my glories Father Yahweh Nissi,

Today hear my worship because of Your love and justice. Lord, I praise You today with songs of psalms. I will also be careful to live a blameless life – I wait for You to come to my aid. Please accept my offering this day as I enter Your gates with thanksgiving and go into Your courts with praise: Give thanks to the Lord, for the Lord is good; Your mercies and kindness endures forever! Thank You Father for Your grace, which is sufficient for me to accomplish Your intended purpose for my life. I thank You that yesterday is behind me, and I forget its woes as well as its triumphs; for today is a present from You and tomorrow no man knows what it holds. So, thank You for the gift that is today; I shall make the most of it with my cooperation to Your will. I thank You for sending Jesus to redeem me from the slavery to sin and eternal death, which was its wage. Thank You for the Holy Spirit, the Teacher and Comforter of my soul. But, more than all of these, I thank You for pre-picking me to save me as one of Your own; for You are Elohim, and You alone will I serve.

Before the mountains were born, before You gave birth to the earth and the world, from the beginning to end, You, El Olam are God. You satisfy us each morning with Your unfailing love, thus I sing for joy to the end of my life. You alone are my refuge, my place of safety, You are my God, Lord Adonai, and I trust You. You cover me with your feathers. You shelter me with your wings. Your faithful promises are my armor of protection. I give thanks to You Lord and proclaim Your unfailing love in the morning, Your faithfulness in the evening, because You are Good. You thrill me, Lord, with all you have done for me! O Lord what great, works that You do! And how deep are Your thoughts. You, O Lord, are King! You are robed in majesty and armed with strength. Your royal laws cannot be changed. Your reign, O Lord his holy forever and ever.

When doubts, fears and unbelief fill my mind, Yahweh Shammah, Your Comfort gives me renewed hope and cheer because You are always there. You are my fortress; You are the Mighty Rock where I hide. I come to You with thanksgiving, and sing You psalms of praise. For You are a great God, a great King above all gods. You, El Roi, hold in Your hands depths of the earth and the mightiest mountain. The sea belongs to You, for You made it, and Your hands also formed the dry land. I come to You with my bowed down worship. I kneel before You Lord, my maker, for You are our God. O Great Shepherd, Yahweh Sabaoth, we are Your people You watch over, the flock under Your care.

Each day I praise Your name and proclaim the good news that You are the Lord who alone can save us. I publish Your glorious deeds among the nations and tell everyone the amazing things You do. Great are You Lord! You are most worthy of praise! You, EL Elyon, are feared above all gods of other nations which are mere idols. Honor and majesty surround You because You made the heavens, and strength and beauty fill Your sanctuary. I love to give You the glory only You deserve; Let all of creation hear my offering whenever I come into Your courts.

Let the trees of the forest rustle with praise before the Lord – Attiq Yomin, for You are coming to judge the earth. You will judge the world with justice and the mountains with Your truth. Fire spreads ahead of You and burns up all Your foes. The heavens proclaim Your righteousness; every nation sees Your glory. Those who worship idols, dear Lord, are disgraced – all who brag about their worthless gods – for every god must bow to You, my El Elyon. For You, O Elohim, are supreme over all the earth; You are exalted far above all gods. Your Right Hand has won a mighty victory; Your Holy Arm has shown Your saving power! Let the sea and everything in it shout Your praise! Let the earth and all living join in – for if they are quiet, You, Lord El Roi, will cause the rocks and stones to praise You!

Lord, El Olam, let me not be counted as the quiet men who do not praise You with my Holy Hands Lifted Up. As for me and my house, we praise Him who sits on His throne between the Cherubim, while the whole earth quakes. I praise Your great and awesome name: YAH-WEH! Your name is holy! Mighty King, lover of justice. You have established fairness and acted with justice. I exalt You Lord God as I bow before Your feet, for You are holy! O Elohim, You performed miraculous signs and wonders in the Land of Egypt – things still re-membered to this day! And You have continued to do great miracles in Israel, and all around the world. You have made Your name famous to this day. This is the day the Lord has made; I will rejoice and be glad in it!

We thank You, El Shaddai, that You are faithful and true to forgive all sins and here and now confess to You each and every one of our sins And thank You for Your faithful forgiveness. We nail our flesh to the cross today, Lord, that our flesh be put to death as our daily sacrifice and obedience to Your Word. And because we died with Christ, the enemy has no authority over the death of our bodies and thus no access to our minds without our permission.

That we here and now revoke that consent given through deception and subject the dictates and lusts of the flesh under our heavenly created spirit; And our spirit, which is always aligned and obedient to Your Spirit, the Spirit who is the creator of time Himself, and because You, Lord Adonai, are not bound by the dispensation of time;

You stepped outside of time, gathered and took every earthly sin, past present and future, all the way from Adam to the last person to ever be born in the future on this earth and imputed them all on Your most excellent sacrificial Lamb during the Calvary Ceremony as the perfect sin offering, who is Christ, when He cried out, as He died for our sins once and for all, "tetelestai", which translates in the Greek – "It is Finished!" and "The bill has been paid."

We thank You Father, that there is no sin that we will ever commit, that You have not already placed upon the head of Christ, making Him the last blood sacrifice ever; therefore, we receive the offer of His free gift of Your Grace dear Lord.

We honor His sacrifice by putting our flesh to death with Him, but also that we share with our regenerated spirit His rise, and joined to His Body as His holy and acceptable unblemished church as we daily renew our minds to the sufficiency of Your Grace. Abba Father, we love You because You first loved us so much that Your Hand in our life's affairs have led us, and keeps us on the path to You.

Abba Father in heaven, You have said, *"Put on the whole armor of God, that we may be able to stand against the wiles of the devil. For we wrestle not against flesh and blood, but against principalities, against powers, against the rulers of darkness of this age, against spiritual hosts of wickedness in heavenly places."* (Ephesians 6:11-12)

As we pray, we place our complete trust in You, Elohim, and Your Word as the word of truth, *as we gird ourselves by taking up the whole armor of God, so that we may be able to withstand in this evil day, and having done all to stand; we stand therefore* in Jesus' Name.

So that the fertile ground of our believing hearts will no longer accept weed seed lies from the unseen spiritual enemy, *we gird our waist with truth*; to assist us in managing the lasting effects of sin is our Advocate, Jesus, who is always pleading our case before You dear Father, the only One who is truly righteous. *We therefore put on the covering breastplate* of Jesus who maintains our right standing with You;

Your Word in Isaiah 52 says, *"How beautiful on the mountains are the feet of the messenger who brings the good news of peace and salvation"*; We therefore, *shod our beautiful feet with the battle preparation of the gospel of peace*;

Lord God, so that we may always be ready to prove our confidence in everything we hope for, we interlock our shield wall with all believing saints in this battle – *above all* – *by taking our shield of NOW-Faith with which we are able to quench all the fiery darts of the wicked one*; And, the crowning authority of our **Positive Throne of Adam** which protects our Subconscious minds from erected strongholds, *we take our helmet of knowing our once-for-all salvation.*

Just as when Jesus, full of the Holy Spirit, returned from the Jordan River was led by the Spirit into the wilderness; where He was tempted by the devil for forty days, He used the incorruptible Word of God as the only offensive weapon needed when He said – 3-times to counter Satan's 3-lies, *"It's written..."* And because **we now know** it is also an unseen enemy who opposes us, and not the people around us - who are also Your children; we too unsheathe the *sword of the Spirit, which is the Word of God,* Jesus;

We thank you Father for this gift of protection and ask You to fulfil Your Word to make Your purpose for this protection during our walk, assignment, purpose and prayer reign in our lives, as we pray always with all prayer and supplication in the spirit, we are watchful to this end with all perseverance and supplication for all saints – and for us also that utterance may be given to us, that we may open our mouths boldly to make known the mystery of the gospel, for which we are ambassadors in chains; that in it we may speak boldly, as we ought to speak; that we do not cease to give thanks for all the saints, making mention of them in our prayers:

"That the God of our Lord Jesus Christ, the Father of Glory, may give you the spirit of wisdom and revelation in the knowledge of Him, the eyes of your understanding being enlightened; that you may know what is the hope of His calling, what are the riches of the Glory of His inheritance in the saints, and what is the exceeding greatness of His power towards us who believe,

According to the working of His mighty power which He worked in Christ when He raised Him from the dead and seated Him at His right hand in the heavenly places, far above all principality and power and might and dominion, and every name that is named, not only in this age but also in that which is to come.

And God has put all things under the authority of Christ and has made Him head over things for the benefit of us, the church. And the church is His body, it is made full and complete by Christ, who fills all things everywhere with Himself." (Ephesians 1:17-23). And by that authority, Christ – The Head, now shares with us – His Body, the **Sovereign Authority Dominion And Might** that restores us to our Adam-ship assignment as given by You Lord in the beginning, in the garden.

Abba Father in heaven, we stand in proxy for Your called ones, Your ADAM-Man, in this prayer of repentance, petition, and warfare cry to You until Your revelation of prayer has reached their hearts and minds and they join in as Interceding Rocks for themselves and their loved ones, in Jesus Name.

Lord El Olam, in the beginning, You blessed the purpose of Your first Adam with Sovereign Authority Dominion And Might over the earth, the fish, vegetation, animals, and all living things. Because he lost that Sovereign Authority Dominion And Might a call from You went out in Genesis 3:9 – "**Adam, (Authority Dominion And Might) Where Are You?**: as You dispatched Your plan and Grace for the Second Adam – the Lord Jesus Christ, to restore and *Remodel* man to former fullness of his Sovereign – ADAM-Man – state of Authority Dominion And Might through the restoration which re-establishes us to our intended wholeness.

Abba Father, thank You for this **Foundation *Remodel*** in these five life areas: **1:) Messiah**, so that we may know Your will, what part in Your will we play, and trust You as our Lord and King as You draw us back to the garden where we find our Sovereign Authority Dominion And Might that You restore back to us when we cry out to Jesus: "*Adam, (Authority Dominion And Might) Where Can I Find You?*"; **2:) Self**, so that You can reveal to us within our spirit, Your will for us, who we are, why You created us and stop "*The Fatherless Son from Wandering*" by directing us to our *Positive Throne of Adam*, renewing our minds, and establishing our stand at the posts of our assignments and purpose; Yahweh Shalom, I now climb up to my watchtower and stand at my guard post, while I wait for You Lord God, to answer my call for Your vision and plan for me.

3:) Proper **Love**, so that we may learn to imitate the very nature of You Elohim, which is to Love, Give, and Sacrifice as shown in Your works as we pray always with *"Holy Hands Lifted Up"* and answer the call to be like You *"Compelled to Compassion"*. **4:) Finances**, so that we may demonstrate impeccable stewardship over the blessing You have empowered us to get wealth and to possess the land that You have instructed us to keep, dress, and multiply, as we occupy as *"Private Money Covenant"* Bankers – *Lending even that which We Borrow*, until Jesus' return;

I especially thank You, Abba Yahweh Nissi, in our all-consuming area of **Finances** and for providing the revelation of Your Divine financial Pre-Paid plan for me to have: The perfect, productive, well-paying career position; Witty ideas and inventions I take all the way to the paying market; Success in all business ventures and *"Private Money Covenant"* contracts; and, Unhindered access to every banker, lender, investor, Secretary of Treasury, IRS Director, Federal Reserve Chairman, US President, and mentor Your Favor has purposed for me – by making a clear and direct path to establish my Godly "There Place", where You are pouring out me a blessing under Your Window of Heaven in this world's economy for my Kingdom Purpose to be fulfilled, in Jesus Name.

And finally, **5:) Family**, to imitate You Father, as *"Interceding Rocks"* to pray, love, and provide leadership to the harvest and our families, as kings and priests, as God's ordained head and leaders of our homes, families, and church body knowing the scriptures so that we may wash our wives, our children, and shepherd Your family of

Wandering sheep back into the safety of the flock by the cleansing of Your Word and the sowing of good seed in their hearts only.

Lord, Yahweh Shalom, Your established order of our **Remodel** is a perfect one, and by Your grace and peace maintains our dignity as men while under Your heavenly re-construction; **Messiah**, **Self**, proper **Love**, **Finances** and **Family**. Father, as Your Word declares: *Proverbs 1:7*, teaches us before there can be us, there is You, it says:

"Fear of the Lord is the foundation of true knowledge", and; *Proverbs 24-27* instructs us Your priority to becoming Your ADAM-Man as well as the proper order You established as best for us; - clarifying the wisdom of producing enough income to care for a wife prior to marring her and starting a family; it reads: - *"Prepare your work outside And get it ready for yourself in the field; Afterward build your house and establish a home."* And *Proverbs 24:3* gives us understanding of exactly how to build a house; and the wisdom to turn it into an eternal Godly home: *"Through [skillful and godly] wisdom a house [a life, a home, a family] is built, And by understanding it is established [on a sound and good foundation]"*.

Dear Heavenly Father, we thank You for this understanding, for in *Proverbs 4:7* You have said in Your word, *"in all of your getting, get understanding"*, and we here and now submit and consent to Your full foundation **Remodel** as we respond to Your – *Genesis 3:9* call from the garden that ends our grouping, stretching, reaching and clawing search through outreached hands back to the waiting Christ, with our own question; **"Authority, Dominion, And Might – Where Can I Find You?"**, in Jesus Name.

We ask, Father what is it that You want, what affairs are on Your holy agenda today that You may download to us to assist You with? What do You want to happen on earth? We thank You Father that

Your blessing is with us in the course of accomplishing Your work on earth.

We thank You Lord Adonai, and ask You Father to fulfil Your word that as we release this and every prayer for each other that we may be healed. We receive this healing here and now in abundance and thank You, that You are faithful and true to do for us whatever You say.

And Father, we pray over our families, these captives in exile, and Your Remodeled ADAM-Man, that You, Yahweh Sabaoth, surround them with Your covenant kindness and covenant protection as a shield for them and all of their loved ones, their wives, their children, one-by-one; and cause them to have blessed victory as we pray for each of them as well as the peace and prosperity of the cities in which You have carried them into exile; that the land prospers so that they too may prosper in accordance with Jeremiah 29:7, and also let each and every one of them find favor in the sight of any official over them for Your sake. Give us Your all-sufficient grace to endure all adversity with patient peace and joy in You, in Jesus Name.

Now Father, we decree and declare by the Sovereign Power of the Eternal Spirit You have given us back through Christ, that we place all power and works of the enemy and his lies under our feet and bruise his head as we join You Jesus, in our seated position of authority as members of Your Body; as we rebuke Satan and revoke all consent that allows his demonic forces to twist Your truth dear Lord, in our minds, in the name of Jesus.

Because we are the godly, in the name of Jesus, we decree and declare that our every step is directed by You Lord; Although we may stumble, we shall never remain fallen because You, Yahweh Shammah, are faithful to confirm Your word – "that although a righteous man falls seven times, he will rise, but the wicked falls once and is destroyed; we are never abandoned by You, Lord El Roi, nor will our children ever beg for bread; thank You Father, that we only give good counsel in Your name and teach what is right and what is wrong.

Now Father, as Your godly Garden *Remodel* project that You are restoring back to **Sovereign Authority Dominion And Might**; one, in which You have deemed as godly, and by that authority, we enforce the mandate of the promised inheritance of our land; that we live with You forever; and we watch as the wicked are destroyed, in the name of Jesus.

El Shaddai, because of Your Shekinah Glory, the enemy who continually opposes us, is now opposed by You; our enemies are now Your enemies; we therefore stand firm in the victory of Jesus over those who war against us by and through the Blood of the innocent lamb, Jesus.

We decree and declare, that since we fear You, Lord God Adonai, Your angel of the Lord is our rear guard, in Jesus name.

Abba Father, You have said, *"command ye My hand"*, and that You personally inhabit the praise of the righteous; therefore Father, hear and inhabit our praise to You right now, confirm Your word, as we now command Your hand – for You, Elohim, to muster Your armor; take up Your shield, lift up Your spear and javelin; prepare for battle, inhibit our praise, and come to our aid;

In the name of Jesus, we declare victory over those who pursue us; we take up our sword of the Spirit, which is the Word of God, and cast down each vain imagination, vex, hex and every high thought that exalts itself, and dares to oppose You and Your knowledge, Dear Father.

In the name of Jesus, we dispatch calamity to overtake the wicked who hate righteousness; and we take our refuge in You dear Lord, because You have redeemed us.

Father, we here and now confirm our covenant, as disciples of Christ, to operate in the **Sovereign Authority Dominion and Might** over the works of Your hands, in both the heavens and the earth that was given back to us by the finished works of Jesus;

We announce our harmonious consent of Your will to make disciples of all nations; to baptize them in the name of the Father, The Son, and The Holy Spirit; by and through Your power, Jesus, and we declare that You are always with us, in Jesus name.

We decree into the heavenlies, that we deny our self-willed - self-life, which is hostile against Your will Father, and take up our cross daily to follow You Jesus; We declare our obedience by laying down our lives for Your sake, where we find Your will and our real spirit-life in You dear Lord; We here and now usurp every part of our will hostile towards You and consent for it to cooperate in harmony with Your will, and thus lay up our profit in heaven, in the name of Jesus.

In the name of Jesus, Father, we place ourselves under Your healing light of truth so that we may discover and know all lies concerning ourselves, our Private Status, our health, our Pre-paid wealth, our Private Equity remedy, our mental state, and physical conditions that we have accepted from evil spirits which have set-up strongholds and citadels in our minds – that continue to trigger sin, poverty and adverse conditions in our lives, so that You may reveal, and help us rid ourselves of every counterfeit thought, idea, attitude, prophecy, and suggestion causing us any vexation, weakness, sickness, brokenness, depression, oppression, impoverished mind-set and/or lack.

Abba Father, we thank You for our regenerated spirit that reconciles us and brings us home to You for all eternity. Now, Yahweh Yireh, so that we may carry out our worldly assignments, we ask You to renew, enlarge and strengthen our minds by shining Your Glory Light and installing our Positive Throne of Adam into the darkened areas of our minds where Lucifer and his evil spirits have established their lies as bases-of-operation, as strongholds, to keep us deceived which we have mistakenly accepted as truth.

In the name of Jesus, we bind their further access and control, and loose Your Word of Truth as our **Positive Throne of Adam** that destroys his footing by replacing them with the full enlightenment of Your will, that we hereby acknowledge and accept, placing our will in cooperation and agreement with You, so that not only our walk, but also our thinking attracts and glorifies You.

We bind every uncontrolled thoughts, imaginations, impure pictures, wanderings, prejudices, and confused ideas that emanate from principalities; from powers; from rulers of darkness of this age; and from spiritual hosts of wickedness in heavenly places that are attempting to inject into – or subtract from – anything to do with our minds.

We further bind any attempt to induce us, through our minds, to accept their "Balak-like" curses, as our own words for us to speak, say our utter over ourselves as these curses intending to thwart Your promises.

Instead, Lord God, may You return them – One-Thousand Fold, back into the enemy's camp as spiritual bombs that explode over them, in the same way Balaam ended up prophesying over *"the apple of Your eye"*, Israel; and never return to us except as the blessing, You have placed in their mouth instead that they must release over us NOW!, in Jesus name.

In the name of Jesus, everything added to our minds by evil spirits is now hereby removed; everything that was subtracted from our minds by them is now added back. We take back our Sovereignty forfeited and all ground given through an un-renewed or improper mind, misunderstanding Your truth, accepting suggestions, or the result of a blank or passive mind – and evict all occupied territory as our minds are renewed by Your revealing light of our **Positive Throne of Adam**, Dear Father.

Because we think for ourselves and resist every satanic lie, whether it be in the form of a thought, suggestion, imagination, or argument, Lucifer and his cohorts must NOW FLEE from us, in Jesus name; and we overthrow these lies, one-by-one, we formally believed – but now disbelieve, by the sprinkling of the blood of the sacrificed innocent Lamb, Jesus; and after which, the smudging of Your anointed oil of wisdom over our ear, thumb, and toe, as well as its pouring over our heads and minds, in Jesus name.

We thank You Father for the gift that is our children, born in our youth, which is to us a reward; We declare that they are our arrows that fill the quiver in our hands; when our accusers confront us at the city gates, we will not be put to shame, in Jesus name.

Ephesians 5:1 instructs us to imitate You, Father, as dear children; As imitating fathers, We declare we do not provoke our children to anger, but bring them up in the discipline and instructions of You Dear Lord, that they may dwell with us in joy and hunger for Your Word as we pray always over our children and grand-children, in Jesus name.

Father, we thank You for Your word in *Proverbs 18:22*; "*He that findeth a wife findeth a good thing, And obtains favor from the Lord.*"

We decree and declare that we will dwell with our wives with understanding, giving honor to her as the weaker vessel, as being heirs together of the grace of life that this and none of our prayers will be hindered, in Jesus name.

We decree and declare that we are compassionate, loving, tenderhearted and of one spirit with our wives, and we bind the enemy from having any further access to our oneness in marriage, in Jesus name.

We place Heaven and Earth on notice that: We are the husbands and fathers God wants us to be. We are led by the Holy Spirit in all decisions. We know how to really love our wives and children. We are delivered from negative behavior. We speak words that build up, and never destroy; Word Seeds that produce life and never death. We possess the desire to always pray for our wives and children. We will continue to grow spiritually, emotionally, and mentally, in Jesus name.

We decree and declare that in us, God has created a clean heart, a renewed mind, and a renewed right spirit, in Jesus name.

We decree and declare that we do not operate in anger, strife or contention, there is no confusion or breech in the spirit between us and our wives and children. We will be immediately convicted by the Holy Spirit of truth anytime we are unforgiving or do not operate as the head of our homes and family and immediately make the change, in Jesus name.

We decree that we love our wives just as Christ loves the church, and we declare that we will give our lives for them, in Jesus name.

In the name of Jesus, we announce and release in the atmosphere that our wives and children are strong in NOW-Faith, they continue to grow spiritually, the spend time in the Word of God, they have discernment and revelation, they are becoming mighty sons and daughters of God, they are a light to others, they know God's will for their lives and live in it daily.

We decree and declare; our wives and children have wisdom and understanding in all areas of business, banking, finance, real estate, insurance and their work, they posses in their hands the power to produce six and seven figure annual incomes so that our wives and daughters may diligently care for our homes and children effortlessly, as Proverbs 31: Women, in our absence, in Jesus name.

Lord, we effect and activate the **Sovereign Authority Dominion And Might** You have given us over all the power of the enemy, and we decree that **Sovereign Authority Dominion And Might** over the unseen spiritual enemy and his lies. We declare that he cannot twist the truth of God in our wives and children's minds another day in their life, in Jesus name.

By the **Sovereign Authority Dominion And Might** given to us, we declare that our wives and children are so solid in the Word of God and in truth that they can immediately identify a lie of the enemy, cast it aside, and listen only to the voice of Yahweh, in Jesus name.

We effect and enforce the mandate of Yahweh Sabaoth's mighty protection over our wives and children. We declare favor where favor is due and supernatural increase is chasing them down, overtaking them and providing abundant supply right NOW, in Jesus name.

In the name of Jesus, we declare that our every prayer asked of You is of one mind with Christ, in NOW-Faith; since we are not double-minded, we receive everything we ask of You because Jesus is right there interceding for us, right now, at Your right hand.

We decree and declare that the Body of Christ, which is us, is rising up together in revival, on one accord, in NOW-Faith, and love, as one glorious Church driven by the power of Jesus Himself, in Jesus name.

I thank You Father, Yahweh Shamma, that You always hear me. In the name of Jesus, I declare that these prayer points take on the characteristics of divine projectiles in the realm of the spirit; and hit their mark.

I bind any retaliation by Satan or any of his cohorts in heaven and earth, in Jesus name.

By the power and the blood, I seal this prayer and loose it in both heaven and earth, in Jesus name.

We ask You Father, El Roi, to fulfill Your Word and make Your purpose reign in our lives. We all have plans and goals that we are pursuing. We ask that You, Yahweh, establish whatever is from You – and cause to fade away whatever is not from You. We honor You as, El Elyon – our creator and as our loving Heavenly Father.

We affirm that it is You who work in us to will and to act according to Your good purposes as in Philippians 2:13. Renew our minds so that we may understand Your ways and Your plans more fully. We pray this in the name of Jesus, who said to Thomas & Andrew, *"I am the way, the truth, and the life, and no one comes to the Father except through me."* (*John 14:6*) And this same Jesus who taught His disciples, instructs us also to always pray this way:

Our Father
Who art in heaven, hallowed be thy name
Thy kingdom come, thy will be done
On earth, as it is in heaven
Give us this day, our daily bread
And forgive us our debts, as we forgive our debtors
And lead us not into temptation, but deliver us from evil
For thine is the kingdom, and the power, and the glory
Forever, and ever

Amen.

"2025 is an incredible Year! Success, Excellent Spiritual and Mental Health, Exceptional Physical Shape, Prosperity, and Abundance in many different forms are Blessing my life this year. I gratefully enjoy and accept their manifestations throughout my life and happily share these blessings of abundance with many others in order to bring happiness to their lives as well."

"I'm Alert – I'm Alive – And I Feel Great!"
"I'm Alert – I'm Alive – And I Feel Great!"
"I'm Alert – I'm Alive – And I Feel Great!"
"My Best of My Days are Still Out in Front of Me"
"I have a Bright Future"
"I Have Found the Second Adam"
"I Have the Favor of God"
"People Like Me"
"God, I Praise You Because You Have Made Me in an Amazing Way. You Have Placed My Blessing, a Gift from You, as An Image of Abundance & Victory Within My Spirit and Subconscious Mind, Which You Have Authorized Me to Manifest. What You Have Done is Your Wonderful Will For My Life – And For That Reason"
"I Accept:"
"That I Am a Victor, and Not a Victim
That I Am Wonderful
That I Am Amazing
That I Am A Masterpiece
That I Am Happy
That I Am Healthy
That I Am Wealthy
That I Am Creative
That I Am Talented
That I Am Valuable

That I Am Secure

That I Am Worthy

That I Am Writer Of Favorable Contracts

That I Am Anointed

That I Am Positive

That I Am Blessed

That I Am Grateful

That I Am Strong

That I Am Beautiful

That I Am Fit

That I Am Confident

That I Am Mighty

That I Am Courageous

That I Attract Money And Opportunities

That I Am Rich

That Money Chases Me Down

That I Am Peace

That I Am Faithful To God

That I Am Blood Covenant Of Abraham, That's Mine Too

That I Will Live 120 Years And Look 30

That I Am Fit With The Body Of A Tuned Athlete

That I Am Healthy Eater

That All Food Eaten Is Healthy, Because I Bless It First

That I Am Wisdom

That I Am Just Like My Father – Love

That I Am A Man After God's Own Heart

That I Am Lender

That I Am The Head

That I Am Above Only

That I Am Established As Holy By God

That I Am Righteous

That I Am Leadership

That I Am Royalty

That I Am Excited About The Blessing That Is Today

That I Am The Standard God Is Raising Against The Flood
Of Satan
That I Repeatedly Call Those Things That Be Not, As
Though They Were; Until They Are, With The NOW-Faith Of
A Mustard Seed, In Jesus Name"
Amen!